## In the Secret Annex

*Our mood is rising,* says Anne, and *everything is going well.* In hiding, they hoped it would all be over. Anne even thought she might be able to go back to school in October. Her hopes rose even further when news of the attempts on Hitler's life became known on July 21, 1944. Anne's reactions are positively euphoric. *I'm finally getting optimistic. Now, at last, things are going well! They really are! Great news! An assassination attempt has been made on Hitler's life, and for once not by Jewish Communists or English capitalists, but by a German general who's not only a count, but young as well. The Führer owes his life to "Divine Providence": he escaped, unfortunately, with only a few major burns and scratches.*

It is impossible to read these passages without a sense of grief and anguish. All Anne Frank's hopes were in vain. The liberation came too late for her.

# OTHER PUFFIN BOOKS YOU MAY ENJOY

# MIRJAM PRESSLER

FOREWORD BY

RABBI HUGO GRYN

TRANSLATED BY

ANTHEA BELL

WITH A NOTE BY

EVA SCHLOSS

# ANNE FRANK

## A
## Hidden
## Life

PUFFIN BOOKS

# For Yola and Noah

PUFFIN BOOKS
Published by the Penguin Group
Penguin Putnam Books for Young Readers,
345 Hudson Street, New York, New York, 10014, U.S.A.
Penguin Books Ltd, 27 Wrights Lane, London W8 5TZ, England
Penguin Books Australia Ltd, Ringwood, Victoria, Australia
Penguin Books Canada Ltd, 10 Alcorn Avenue, Toronto, Ontario, Canada  M4V 3B2
Penguin Books (N.Z.) Ltd, 182-190 Wairau Road, Auckland 10, New Zealand

Penguin Books Ltd, Registered Offices: Harmondsworth, Middlesex, England

First published in Germany by Beltz Verlag, Weinham and Basel, as *Ich Sehne Mich
So: Die Lebensgeschichte der Anne Frank*, 1992
Published in Great Britain by Macmillan Children's Books, London, 1999
First published in the United States of America by Dutton Children's Books,
a division of Penguin Putnam Books for Young Readers, 2000
Published by Puffin Books, a division of Penguin Putnam Books for Young Readers, 2001

1   3   5   7   9   10   8   6   4   2

The foreword by Rabbi Hugo Gryn first appeared in *The Diary of Anne Frank*, published in 1995
by Macmillan Children's Books, London, and is reproduced with the permission of Naomi Gryn.
Original text copyright © Beltz Verlag, Weinham and Basel, 1992
Translation copyright © Macmillan Children's Books, 1999
Foreword copyright © The Estate of Rabbi Hugo Gryn, 1995
Author's note and postscript copyright © Mirjam Pressler, 1999
Interior photos copyright © The Anne Frank-Fonds, Basel, and Cosmopress, Geneva, 1999
Jacket photographs copyright © The Anne Frank-Fonds, Basel/Anne Frank Stichting,
Amsterdam, 1999
Translated from German by Anthea Bell
All rights reserved

THE LIBRARY OF CONGRESS HAS CATALOGED THE DUTTON EDITION AS FOLLOWS:
Pressler, Mirjam
[*Ich sehne mich so!* English]
Anne Frank: a hidden life / by Mirjam Pressler; foreword by Rabbi Hugo
Gryn; translated by Anthea Bell; with a note from Eva Schloss
p.  cm.
Includes bibliographical references and index.
Summary: Describes the background in which Anne Frank's life and diary were
set as she hid in an attic in Nazi-occupied Holland for two years.
ISBN 0-525-46330-5
1. Frank, Anne, 1929–1945. Achterhuis.
2. Jews—Persecutions—Netherlands—Amsterdam—Juvenile literature.
3. Jewish children in the Holocaust—Netherlands—Amsterdam—Juvenile literature.
4. Frank, Anne, 1929–1945—Family—Juvenile literature. 5. Amsterdam (Netherlands)—Ethnic
relations—Juvenile literature. [1. Frank, Anne, 1929-1945. 2. Jews—Netherlands—Biography.
3. Holocaust, Jewish (1939-1945)—Netherlands—Amsterdam. 4. Women—Biography.] 1. Title.
DS135.N6F73513  940.53'18'092  [B]  99-089604

Puffin Books ISBN 0-14-131226-2

Printed in the United States of America

# Contents

# Rabbi Hugo Gryn

I once had coffee and cake in a quiet London suburb in the company of Otto Frank and our mutual friend, Rabbi Leo Baeck. Dr. Baeck was one of the great spirits to come through the Holocaust, and we agreed that our survival had nothing to do with our goodness or being clever or having deep religious faith. Many who were infinitely better and wiser and more pious perished. It was a chance thing, but survival placed on us a painful responsibility to speak of our experiences. That Otto Frank spared no effort and managed to overcome every obstacle to get Anne Frank's diary published fulfilled that obligation and gave a measure of meaning not only to her life but also to her death. I shall always be glad that on that summer afternoon I was able to say this to her father in person.

On Wednesday, April 5, 1944, Anne Frank herself wrote to Kitty (the fictitious character to whom she addressed the entries in her diary) and, as it turned out, to us as well: "I want to go on living even after my death!" In that same month, during the festival of Passover, which celebrates the exodus of the Jews from slavery in Egypt, and a few hundred miles east of Amsterdam in my Carpathian hometown of Beregszasz, my

# Foreword

own family and I, and all the Jews in our district, were rounded up. We were forced into a temporary ghetto and very soon made to board those cattle-wagons of the train that took us, not to the promised "agricultural work in the East," but to those fearful lines at Auschwitz-Birkenau, where armed guards and white-coated doctors motioned each person either toward the gas chambers or the similar-looking shower-rooms, which offered the possibility of a little more life beyond as a slave laborer.

Not much later, in the following September, the betrayed Frank family and all those who inhabited the Secret Annex and whom we meet in the pages of the *Diary* also reached this dreadful destination. Though I was a young prisoner myself, not quite fourteen years old, I realized and experienced the starkest evidence of what happens when God is dethroned and replaced by evil principles harnessed to modern technology.

In the intervening years, I have often thought how Auschwitz-Birkenau was the denial and the perversion of all the Ten Commandments, which stand for what we have come to call the Judeo-Christian spiritual tradition and morality—and one of the pillars of Western civilization.

In the Nazi empire, with its direct links between the pomp of Berlin and Berchtesgaden (where so many of Europe's leaders came to be entertained by Hitler and to applaud his plans and program) and the unspeakable terror of the camps of Auschwitz-Birkenau and Bergen-Belsen, it was clear that:

**I *You shall have no other gods before me.***
**God was replaced by a Führer and his minions who claimed for themselves the power of life and death.**

**II  *You shall not make for yourself an idol.***

They fashioned countless idols of silver and gold and filled their world with the sight of swastikas, the sound of *Heil Hitler!*, and the smell of burning corpses.

**III  *You shall not make wrongful use of the name of the Lord your God.***

They swore falsely and made lies an instrument of state policy.

**IV  *Remember the Sabbath day, and keep it holy.***

They created camps of slavery in which the hours of light were spent in forced labor and the darkness filled with loneliness and relentless hunger. In some of the camps I inhabited, the few workless hours were set aside for ritual punishment-beatings.

**V  *Honor your father and your mother.***

Children were made to watch the humiliation and debasement of their parents—and parents had children torn from their arms. Families were desecrated.

**VI  *You shall not murder.***

Murder was at the heart of that culture, and killers were promoted and honored.

**VII  *You shall not commit adultery.***

There was a reward for the betrayal of relationships, and sexual abuse was rife.

**VIII  *You shall not steal.***

Stealing and looting were sanctioned on every level of Nazidom right down to gold teeth and fillings extracted from corpses.

**IX  *You shall not bear false witness against your neighbor.***

Truth was the first and permanent casualty of the system.

# Foreword

**X *You shall not covet your neighbor's goods.***
Covetousness, envy, and unchecked greed became part of
the way of life. Neither person nor property was respected.
The spoilers' appetite for spoils knew no limits.

In those final days of the war and in the first few weeks after
liberation in May 1945, I had many doubts and only one certainty. The doubts were very similar to those of Anne Frank
in the *Diary* itself, and those I imagine her having in
Auschwitz-Birkenau and Bergen-Belsen. Would we survive?
Would any other members of the family survive? Would it be
possible to go back to school? Lead a normal life? Eat and
drink and laugh again? Find the will to rebuild schools and
synagogues and communities? Make an end once and for all
to Jewish powerlessness, which made the scale and extent of
this tragedy possible in the first place?

The single certainty was that when the world saw the enor-
mity of the tragedy that was perpetrated in the name of religious intolerance and racism with its unleashing of such
all-consuming hatreds, that then there would surely never
again be any kind of anti-Semitism or Jew-hatred, nor any
form of victimization of Gypsies or persecution of religious or
political dissenters. But how wrong that solitary certainty of
mine proved to be! Half a century later racists rampage again,
"ethnic cleansing" is talked about and practiced, and in a host
of violent conflicts God's image is desecrated and the memory
and sacrifice of Anne Frank and her generation are betrayed
in far too many places.

I think of Anne Frank and the other one and a half million
Jewish children who perished with her, of the great literature

and many insights that Anne might have produced, and of the
children and grandchildren she might have had. At every
*Yizkor*, or memorial service, I weep as I think of my own
brother, Gabi, and all those children, and of all the love and
learning and laughter that died with them. I think of the
homes they might have built, the illnesses they might have
cured, the decencies that could have been performed, and
how civilization could have been strengthened. I am also conscious of the kind of hope that permeated so much of Anne
Frank's life—and in a way I hope with her, and for her, that
hearts, minds, and attitudes may yet alter and change. That
suspicions and hatred and violence born of differences in
creed or color of skin will be left behind—buried with everything that is so shameful in this most complicated of cen-
turies.

As her *Diary* continues to be read around the world, Anne
Frank's wish to go on living even after her death is also fulfilled, and in ways she could not have anticipated. Nor will
she ever age. She will always remain a young sister and
daughter, and Kitty's trusted friend.

It would have been impossible to predict the events to
which Anne Frank's *Diary* has led. In the years since having
coffee and cake with Otto Frank, I have arranged the pre-
miere of the movie version of the *Diary* while living in Bom-
bay, participated in the opening of the "Anne Frank in the
World Exhibition 1929–1945" in schools and cathedrals in
England, introduced specially choreographed dances reflect-
ing her thoughts and feelings, and even selected excerpts
from the *Diary* that are now included in the prayer books
used by the synagogues I serve. I believe that Anne Frank's

great work will survive her century and ours and remain a timeless testament to the goodness of the human spirit as well as to the destructive reality of evil.

Moments before the Germans entered Kovno in Lithuania in 1940, the head of its *yeshiva*, or rabbinic college, Rabbi Nachum Yanchiker, called together the students and asked them to do everything possible to save their lives. He also charged them with this mandate: "Do not become embittered by waiting and tears. Speak with calmness and serenity, and do as our holy Sages have done—pour forth words and cast them into letters. Then the holy souls of your brothers and sisters will remain alive. These evil ones schemed to blot out their names from the face of the earth; but a man cannot destroy letters. For words have wings; they mount up to the heavenly heights and they endure for eternity."

Anne Frank did not know Rabbi Nachum in person or even by reputation, yet she did exactly what her time and her generation demanded. I believe that her words will continue to testify to decency and natural goodness, and that they will reach hearts and minds for countless generations to come. And that they may indeed endure for eternity.

*Rabbi Hugo Gryn was a well-known commentator on Jewish affairs, senior rabbi of the West London Synagogue, and a survivor of Auschwitz. He died in 1996.*

## A NOTE BY
# Eva Schloss

I liked *Anne Frank: A Hidden Life* very much. It adds some more information about Anne's life and background and also explains certain chapters of the *Diary*.

Reading this book has also brought back many memories, including this one:

In the early 1960s a young couple visited Otto Frank and my mother in their house in Birsfelden, Switzerland. They wanted to know about the writer Gustav Janouch, who lived in Prague. He had translated Anne's *Diary* into Czech and had also written a book about Kafka. The couple told Otto that they intended to visit the writer and Otto said, "I am sure Gustav will ask you to smuggle his Kafka manuscript to the West. This will be very dangerous. Don't do it. *No book, even a very important one, is worth a human life.*"

Clearly, Otto was thinking also of his daughter's diary. How often must he have wished to be able to exchange her life for the success of her work!

He had to live with this reality in all its cruelty. What helped him to do so was the hope that the memory of millions of Holocaust victims might be turned from a senseless

# A Note by Eva Schloss

tragedy into a source of harmony amongst mankind, and that the message of Anne's *Diary* would make an important contribution.

*Eva Schloss*
*Trustee of the Anne Frank Educational Trust UK*

*Eva Schloss and her mother, Elfriede "Fritzi" Geiringer, both survived Auschwitz. In 1953 Elfriede Geiringer married Otto Frank; she died in 1998.*

# Author's Note

The kind of biography I like best shows what a person's life was really like by comparison with what it might have been. It shows which of that person's needs, gifts, and longings were encouraged and which were suppressed; which decisions were made and for what reasons. That is what interests me about the life of Anne Frank—and yet it is far from easy to look at her in that way. Anne Frank did not even live to be sixteen. Many of the events of her life were forced upon her; she had little chance to make her own decisions. She was a girl from a prosperous middle-class family; she was Jewish; and when she was four years old a regime was elected to power in Germany, her home country, that wanted her dead and eventually killed her.

I therefore have to see the story of Anne's life in the light of the history of her time—a time when it was not easy to be anything but a victim or a victimizer.

It is equally important for me to feel involved with Anne herself; she comes to life every time I read her diaries. Her letters to Kitty seem to be addressed to us, her readers; they want us to respond to them, and I think it is impossible not

xvi     to. I am sometimes surprised to find how much Anne's personal development had in common with that of many other young people. Sometimes I feel almost irritated because she takes herself so seriously, and then again I am glad she *did* take herself seriously. Sometimes she seems very far away, when I think of the worlds dividing us. Sometimes she seems as close as if she were my daughter—for my own daughters were also born Jewish, in Germany, but in a better time than hers.

*Mirjam Pressler*

# ANNE FRANK
### A
### Hidden
### Life

# 1 The Liberation

## "ONE DAY WE SHALL BE HUMAN BEINGS AGAIN AND NOT JUST JEWS"

Today it is difficult for us even to imagine what Auschwitz concentration camp must have been like on the day it was liberated. We have never experienced anything like it. Auschwitz was built by the Nazis for the imprisonment and systematic killing of their perceived enemies—mostly Jews but also Gypsies, gay men and women, members of the resistance, prisoners of war, and others. Gas chambers were constructed for these industrialized killings, which began in 1941 and continued until just before the Russians liberated the camp in the last year of World War II.

Otto Wolken, a Jewish doctor from Vienna who was a prisoner in the men's quarantine camp of Auschwitz-Birkenau, has written about his own experiences of the last few days at Auschwitz.[1] Like Otto Frank, Anne Frank's father, he was one of the survivors.

The night of January 17, 1945, was dark and wintry, with snow lying everywhere. The front line was coming closer, and for the last day or so the noise of battle had often been audible. Now it had stopped. The loud banging of a gong was suddenly heard, and shouting. From a hiding place, Otto Wolken

4    watched as the healthier prisoners were rounded up, counted, and marched away. He heard the iron gate of the camp close behind them, chains rattling, the lock snapping shut. He realized that the Allies must be quite close now, and slowly he began to hope: after almost seven years of internment in several German concentration camps, he might perhaps get out of this death factory alive. Like all the others, however, he was afraid the Nazis might try to kill their surviving prisoners at the very last minute.

A little later he was ordered to make lists: a list of men who though sick were strong enough for a ten-mile march, a list of men who could walk the three miles to Auschwitz railway station, and a list of men who could not walk at all. The seriously ill were panic-stricken. None of them wanted to stay in the camp, and they wept and begged him to list them as fit to march. He urged them to stay where they were and promised not to leave them.

When the order came for him to take all papers and documents to the office, Wolken hesitated. Only certain permitted causes of death, such as "heart disease," "pneumonia," or "shot attempting to escape," were entered on the official reports, but Dr. Wolken had made secret notes on the real causes of death of many of the prisoners: "died of starvation," "killed," "died under torture," "gassed." He did not want to part with these documents, so he took only the official casenotes to the office, where they were burned at once. Meanwhile, he hid his own important secret notes.[2]

Then the doctors and nurses were told to get ready to leave. Dr. Wolken decided not to go, believing he stood no chance of surviving a long march. What was more, he had saved an Italian boy from death in the gas chamber and knew

that the boy could not march far in the knee-deep snow; he 5
would have to carry him, and he could not do that for long.
He himself weighed only eighty-three pounds. Finally he hid
under a dying man's straw mattress and waited to see what
would happen next. Not until everything was quiet again did
he come out to organize some kind of emergency medical
care for the sick men left in the quarantine camp. There were
more than two thousand of them.

On the same day, an Allied air raid destroyed the power station in the town of Auschwitz. The camp now had no electric
light and no water, and the chances of surviving the next few
days became much worse. Some of the prisoners who were
still reasonably physically fit dug out two cisterns, or reser-
voirs, under the snow, which lay two feet deep. They cut
holes in the wire fence so that they could make a break for it
if necessary, and broke into the stores searching for food and
finding bread, tea, sugar, and flour.

But the SS* had not left the camp yet; there were still some
guards around. At one point over the next few days, a detachment of security men suddenly appeared when a Russian prisoner of war found a gun and fired some celebratory shots into
the air. They could not find the Russian who had fired the
shots, so they rounded up all Russian prisoners of war still in
the camp, made them stand on the edge of a pit, and shot
them. That evening, SS men set fire to the part of the camp
known as "Kanada."† Its huts were crammed with household

---

* SS: short for *Schutzstaffel*: Defense Unit. The SS began as Hitler's personal body-
guard but grew in numbers and power until it was a huge military and policing organization for carrying out Nazi policies.
† "Kanada" was the name given to the huts in Auschwitz-Birkenau where personal
belongings taken from prisoners in the camp, and those killed on arrival, were
stored, sorted, and prepared for dispatch elsewhere.

6   linen and clothes. The prisoners threw water from their food bowls over the roofs of the huts closest to Kanada, to protect them from the fire and flying sparks. They also took clothing for the sick from the burning storerooms. Luckily, in the morning the wind changed and the risk of the huts catching fire was over.

However, the SS had not given up yet. The next day they assembled machine guns, and an SS guard took up position at the front and back entrance of each block. There was a tense, menacing silence in the camp. But then the guns were dismantled once more and the SS men drove off in a truck. They came back on January 24, this time to take away the last of the Jews in the camp. Wolken tried to hide in a block housing Polish prisoners, but the Poles threw him out, telling him, "This is an Aryan block!" He hid in the sewage of a latrine pit.

On the night of January 26, a loud explosion broke the silence. The SS had blown up Crematorium V to destroy all evidence of what had been going on,[3] that they had sent millions to die in gas chambers and then burned their bodies in crematoria. Around two o'clock the next afternoon, two muffled figures came trudging down the road through the camp in the snow, pulling a machine gun on a sleigh behind them. On their fur caps were the red stars of the Soviet Army. The concentration camp of Auschwitz, whose name was to become a synonym for mass murder and inhumanity, had ceased to exist.

On the evening of that day, January 27, 1945, hundreds of military vehicles drove into the camp. The Soviet Army freed the sick and exhausted prisoners still there. One Russian officer, speaking Yiddish, promised that everything possible would be done to provide them with food and give the sick

the care they needed. The next day the prisoners had soup
with pieces of meat in it; they could hardly even remember
what meat tasted like. Doctors and nurses came into the camp
too. Despite their efforts, thousands who had survived the
camp itself died from the effects of their imprisonment in the
period just after liberation.

The concentration camp of Auschwitz had been built in
1940 on the orders of SS Reich Leader Heinrich Himmler.
"Planet Auschwitz," "Hell," the "Death Factory" ceased to exist on January 27, 1945. There are no reliable statistics for the
numbers of people murdered in Auschwitz alone.[4] The big
German *Brockhaus Encyclopaedia* says that "Millions—particularly Jews—were murdered in Auschwitz up to the occupation of the camp by Soviet troops on January 27, 1945."[5]

How impersonal that word "millions" sounds! It conceals
the fact—only too easily and perhaps too readily forgotten
when round figures of victims are listed—that the murdered
people were all individuals with their own lives to lead. And
one wonders why the encyclopedia says the camp was "occupied" rather than "liberated" by Soviet troops. The word "occupied" sounds rather as if the Soviet troops were doing
something wrong, like the Germans did when they occupied
the Netherlands. What the Soviet Army did at Auschwitz was
very different.

The historian Martin Gilbert, who has studied the history of Auschwitz (and the inadequate Allied response to
the genocide that was going on), says that the Soviet troops
found 650 corpses and about 7,600 survivors: 1,200 in the
main Auschwitz camp, 5,800 (including 4,000 women) in
Auschwitz-Birkenau, and 650 in Monowitz, which belonged
to Auschwitz and was a labor camp operated by the industrial

8     company IG Farben.[6] These figures are also made up of individuals: one of the prisoners liberated was Otto Frank, Anne's father.

What can he have felt that day? Joy, relief, a sense of deliverance? Many prisoners said later that they felt numb when they were liberated and did not experience the incredible happiness they had expected. They realized that their survival did not give them back the lives from which they had been torn when the gates of hell closed behind them. These half-starved prisoners, most of them sick, were neither physically nor mentally in any state to feel exuberant emotions like joy and happiness, quite apart from the fact that they did not know what the immediate future held for them, which of their family and friends were still alive, or if any of them were alive at all. Most of them had nowhere to go; they had lost their homes, their prospects, and their hopes. They were in every sense "displaced persons," the term later used to describe them.

It must have been much the same for Otto Frank. He had lost his original home country of Germany when Hitler first came to power, and he would surely have lost much of his hope in Auschwitz. He must have gone around the camp desperately searching for his wife, his daughters, or the others who had been in hiding with him back in Holland. He found no one. He had last seen Peter van Pels before the SS took the boy away on January 16, on one of the so-called evacuation marches.*

---

* As the Red Army approached, the Nazis tried to "evacuate" their surviving prisoners from concentration camps in the East and move them to camps in Germany or Austria. The evacuation marches were later called "death marches," since anyone who could walk no farther, anyone who even stumbled and fell, was shot without mercy by the accompanying SS guards and left by the roadside.

Otto Frank had tried to persuade Peter to hide in one of the huts used as infirmaries, but Peter had decided that as he was in fairly good health he would go on the evacuation march. When Auschwitz was liberated Otto Frank did not know—and only found out much later—that Peter had indeed survived what would be more accurately called a "death march" and was still alive at the time of the camp's liberation, but died on May 5, 1945, at the camp of Mauthausen in Austria, three days before the Allies got there.

Like all the other prisoners, Otto Frank was horribly emaciated and probably wouldn't have been able to think very clearly or imaginatively. He would have been obsessed by the thought of "going home" to find his wife and daughters, who with luck might have survived. "Home" meant the Netherlands and the building in Amsterdam where he had lived in hiding with his family and four other people from July 1942 until the fateful day of their arrest on August 4, 1944, and where his firm also had its offices. Finally, "home" also meant the helpers who had cared for him and his companions in hiding for more than two years, at the utmost risk to themselves: Miep and Jan Gies, Victor Kugler, Johannes Kleiman, and Bep Voskuijl.

It would be wrong to think that when the soldiers arrived to liberate Auschwitz they were immediately followed by the Red Cross and other relief organizations, distributing food and medicine, setting up hospitals, organizing transport home. It wasn't like that, although the Soviet soldiers did what they could for the survivors. Fritzi Frank, Otto Frank's second wife and a fellow Auschwitz survivor, described their efforts.[7] They sawed the three-tiered bunk beds apart to spare their feeble occupants' having to clamber up. They dug la-

10   trines, since all the lavatories were blocked up and frozen. Any of the freed prisoners who were physically fit enough helped with peeling potatoes and any attempts that could be made at laundry work. For the moment, however, organized transport back to their own countries was out of the question, since the war was not over yet. The two main front lines of fighting, the Eastern Front and the Western Front, now passed right through Germany and were coming closer and closer to each other. There were Allied air raids all the time. Germany was in flames.

Some of the freed prisoners set off home, either on their own or with groups of people from the same country. They set out from the camp and dispersed in all directions through war-torn Europe, many of them in search of relations who might possibly have survived. Others had already given up hope and just wanted to get away from the hell that had been Auschwitz. Soviet soldiers helped them on their way, finding them houses whose owners had fled and where they could stay for a while, or giving them food. The liberated prisoners walked, hitched lifts in army vehicles for part of the way, or were occasionally able to catch a train. They often had to break their journey, either because one could not cross the frontiers between occupation zones without formalities, or because they were still so sick. They were ill, or they fell ill, as a result of starvation, the dreadful conditions in the camps, and even from eating food they weren't used to. The Yiddish writer K. Zetnik, another Auschwitz survivor, describes how a group of liberated prisoners died in terrible agony after eating bacon. Their emaciated, tormented bodies could no longer digest fat.[8]

Otto Frank stayed in the camp until a train set off for

Odessa on March 5. On the way, in Katowice, he met Mrs. de Wiek, whom he had known in Westerbork, the Jewish "assembly camp" in the Netherlands. She had been deported to Auschwitz with him and the others. Otto Frank learned from her that his wife, Edith, had died in the infirmary hut of Auschwitz-Birkenau, with Mrs. de Wiek at her side. However, all she knew about the Franks' daughters was that they had been taken away. "Mr. Frank didn't move when I told him that. I tried to look at his face but he had turned it away, and then he made a movement. I don't remember what movement it was, but I think he laid his head down on the table."9

In the train, Otto Frank met Elfriede (Fritzi) Geiringer, who had fled with her family from Vienna to Amsterdam and had later been deported to Auschwitz. Like Peter van Pels, her husband and son had been on one of the "evacuation marches" and they had "perished" just before the camp was liberated. She and her daughter had survived. (Later, in 1953, she married Otto Frank.) The former prisoners were taken by sea from Odessa to Marseilles, arriving on May 27.

In early June Otto Frank arrived back in Amsterdam, the city he had left barely a year before. There had been eight of them then: Otto Frank, his wife Edith, and their two daughters Margot and Anne, as well as Hermann and Auguste van Pels, their son Peter, and the dentist Fritz Pfeffer.* Eight Jews who had escaped from Germany to the Netherlands, where the Nazis finally caught up with them.

But now Otto Frank was alone. He went to see two people

---

* In her diary, Anne used pseudonyms for her companions in hiding. I am using their real names in this book, while keeping the pseudonyms in the quotations from Anne's diary, where Hermann and Auguste van Pels are called Hans and Petronella van Daan, and Fritz Pfeffer is Albert Dussel.

12    who had proved themselves true friends over the last few
years—Miep and Jan Gies. Perhaps he hoped to find his
daughters with them—after all, Margot and Anne had been
young and healthy and could have survived. Or perhaps he
wouldn't even allow himself to think like that. He went to see
Miep and Jan, but his daughters were not there and there was
no news of them. However, no news might be good news,
since it left room for hope, and he clung to that. "I have great
hope for Margot and Anne," he told Miep.[10]

Miep and Jan Gies welcomed Otto Frank into their home,
gave him a room, and cared for him. Disciplined and self-
controlled as always, he went back to his firm. He had not
been able to enter its offices for years, not since he himself
had "Aryanized" it* with a prudent eye to the future. Work is
a distraction and creates a sense of normality, but what can
Otto Frank have felt like after his terrible experiences in
Auschwitz—after seeing appalling murders and starvation?
How can he have concentrated again on selling pectin to
housewives for making jam? Did he see the grotesque side of
the situation, or was he just glad to be living a "normal" life
once more with a job to distract him? Besides working, he
tried desperately to find out what had happened to the people
who had been in hiding with him. He went to all the different
refugee committees, searching the lists of victims' names that
had been compiled from information given by survivors,
afraid he would find the names of Margot and Anne Frank.

Then, one day, news came that destroyed all hope: Margot

---

* In Nazi jargon, to "Aryanize" a firm or a business meant forcing Jewish owners to
"sell" their possessions to Aryans—non-Jews, people of "Nordic" descent. The term
conceals what was actually the looting and seizure of the property of the former
owners. Such measures were intended to "de-Judaize" the economy.

and Anne would not be coming back either. They had both perished in Bergen-Belsen.

(The word usually used at the time was "perished"—in German *umgekommen*—but Anne and Margot were without doubt murdered, although they died of exhaustion and typhus and no one actually shot them with his own hands or forced them into a gas chamber. Unfortunately, there is no good term to describe the creation of conditions in which the death of human beings is not just allowed but deliberately intended. The nonexistent phrase should be something like "armchair murder.")

Two sisters, Janny Brandes-Brilleslijper and Lien Rebling-Brilleslijper, had survived Auschwitz and Bergen-Belsen. They had known Anne and Margot and reported their deaths to the Red Cross. Janny remembers the day when Otto Frank visited them. "Much later, in the summer of 1945, a tall, thin, distinguished man stood on the sidewalk. He looked through our window and Bob opened the door. [. . .] And there stood Otto Frank. He asked if I knew what had happened to his two daughters. I knew, but it was hard to get the words out of my mouth. He had already heard from the Red Cross, but he wanted to have it confirmed. [ . . .] He took it very hard. He was a man who didn't show his feelings openly, he had tremendous self-control."[11]

Miep Gies tells us that after Otto Frank had heard the news from the Red Cross he walked slowly into his office. Miep herself took Anne's diaries from a drawer in her desk where she had kept them since August 4, 1944. They had been waiting for Anne, but now Anne would never come home. According to Miep's own account, she took all the notes, the autograph album, the exercise books, the accounts book, the

14    loose sheets, carried them into Otto Frank's room, gave them
      to him, and said, "Here is your daughter Anne's legacy to
      you."[12]

      This remark, with all its pathos, seems to me to have been
      colored by later events and emotions. I can imagine Miep feel-
      ing shattered, perhaps crying, and wondering whether this
      was the moment to give Otto Frank his daughter's writings, or
      if it would be better to wait. I imagine her looking for the ex-
      ercise books and loose sheets, piling them up, and then, still
      unsure of herself, taking them to his office, giving him the pa-
      pers, and saying at most one or two words—"From Anne" or
      "Anne's diaries." And now, if not before, beginning to weep.

# 2 The Diaries

## "AFTER THE WAR I'D LIKE TO PUBLISH A BOOK"

The original Dutch edition of Anne Frank's diaries, *Het Achterhuis* ("The Annex"), and its translations into other languages, including the English-language edition, *The Diary of a Young Girl*, is not a diary kept in chronological order from beginning to end as one might expect. The main part of the book consists of a second version of Anne's original diary, revised with additions by Anne herself, with some stories from the accounts book in which she also wrote.

Anne Frank had lived in the Netherlands since she was four years old, so although she was born German she wrote in Dutch; the history of her diaries and their translations is fascinating not just to literary critics but to anyone interested in the way a book comes into being: fascinating because we can follow Anne Frank's progress from the naïve teenager who begins writing the diary to the real writer she became later, and all in not much more than two years.

Anne Frank was given her first diary—in fact an autograph album with a red, orange, and gray checked cover—for her thirteenth birthday on June 12, 1942. At this time the family was still living in the Merwedeplein in Amsterdam, more or

16    less at liberty, although their freedom was considerably re-
stricted by the many anti-Jewish laws and regulations imposed by the German occupying forces. Anne received many
gifts for her thirteenth birthday, but the diary, as she writes,
was *maybe one of my nicest presents.** It is noticeable that in
her very first entry on the flyleaf she is already addressing it
directly, as a person: *I hope I will be able to confide everything
to you, as I have never been able to confide in anyone, and I hope
you will be a great source of comfort and support.*[13] The diary is
"you," someone to talk to, a friend with whom she develops a
personal relationship. Later she gave it a name, Kitty.

Until he came back from Auschwitz, Otto Frank had never
read his daughter's diary. Everyone in the Secret Annex and
all the helpers had known she was writing one, but none of
them had seen it. She might sometimes have read a passage or
one of her stories aloud; we know she read passages to Mrs.
van Pels and Peter. She gave her father her story "The Fairy"[14]
for his birthday in 1944. Anne mentions a conversation with
Margot about a suggestion that they might let each other read
parts of their diaries sometime, but nothing seems to have
come of it; at least, Anne does not refer to the subject again.

We can only guess at Otto Frank's emotions when he read
the diaries. Already grieving over his daughter's death, he
must have felt even more distressed when he realized that he
had known only the surface Anne—the side she was ready to
show the world. He did not know the second Anne, who was
*much purer, deeper and finer*, nor did any of the people with
whom she had lived at such close quarters for more than two

---

* Throughout the book, passages from Anne's diary are indicated by italics.

years, for she herself had hidden that other Anne from them.
Her father may have had some idea of his daughter's hidden
personality, but he did not know it very well or he would
hardly have responded in such an injured way to the letter in
which she defended her independence and her determination
to be responsible for herself (see the entries of May 5 and 7,
1944).

The first diary is written in the autograph album mentioned above and runs from June 12, 1942, to December 5 of
the same year. Later on Anne made a few additions to some of
the entries, and because of the paper shortage she went back
to use some pages that she had left empty. The next diary to
have been preserved is an exercise book with a black binding,
covered in brown wrapping paper; it begins on December 22,
1943, over a year after her last entry in the first diary. As she
certainly did not stop writing during that year, we have to assume that at least one volume of the diary is lost. The third
preserved diary is in another exercise book, with a green and
gold spotted binding and again covered in brown wrapping
paper, and it begins on April 17, 1944. The last entry is for
August 1, 1944.

Thanks to what are usually called the "loose sheets," we
know what happened between December 1942 and December
1943 even though the diary covering that period is lost. The
reason for the existence of the loose sheets can be traced back
to a talk on Radio Oranje. When the Germans occupied Holland in May 1940, the Queen of the Netherlands took refuge
in London, where a government in exile was set up. Over Radio Oranje it broadcast news and appeals to the Dutch people
to stand firm. On March 28, 1944, the Minister of Education,

18 Art, and Science in the government in exile gave an address in which he said, "History cannot be written on the basis of official decisions and documents alone. If our descendants are to understand fully what we as a nation have had to endure and overcome during these years, then what we really need are ordinary documents—a diary, letters from a worker in Germany, a collection of sermons given by a parson or a priest. Not until we succeed in bringing together vast quantities of this simple, everyday material will the picture of our struggle for freedom be painted in its full depth and glory."[15] The minister spoke of a national center where the material to be collected could be edited and published. (Such a center was indeed set up later as the Rijksinstituut voor Oorlogsdocumentatie, the Netherlands State Institute for War Documentation, which published the Critical Edition* of the *Diary of Anne Frank* in 1986.)

Anne and the others in hiding had been listening to the minister's address, and the next day, on March 29, 1944, she wrote in her diary: *Of course, everyone pounced on my diary. Just imagine how interesting it would be if I were to publish a novel about the Secret Annex. The title alone would make people think it was a detective story. Seriously, though, ten years after the war people would find it very amusing to read how we lived, what we ate and what we talked about as Jews in hiding.*

On May 11, 1944, she wrote: *And now something else. You've known for a long time that my greatest wish is to be a journalist,*

---

* A critical edition is a comprehensive scholarly version of a text showing all surviving earlier stages of its creation. All drafts of the wording are included, with the author's notes and revisions, and the variants are printed side by side. A critical edition also contains comments on the books and documents used by the author, etc. Unlike a straightforward reading edition, it illustrates all phases in the creation of the text and shows how the author worked.

*and later on, a famous writer. We'll have to wait and see if these grand illusions (or delusions!) will ever come true, but up to now I've had no lack of topics. In any case, after the war I'd like to publish a book called* The Secret Annex. *It remains to be seen whether I'll succeed, but my diary can serve as the basis.*

Then she began work on her book, *The Secret Annex*, and this brings us to the "loose sheets." Paper was in short supply, so she got hold of some flimsy copy paper of the kind used in office typewriters, probably provided by Miep or Bep, another one of the helpers. She began copying out her own diaries on these flimsy sheets. As she worked, she rearranged the entries, sometimes adding several letters of different dates to one that previously stood on its own, cutting, expanding, leaving out uninteresting entries (or entries that she thought uninteresting), writing new passages that cast light on something. Thus there was a second version of her diaries, which she hoped to publish later. Today it is known as version B.

The revised version includes the missing year, so at the time Anne must still have had the volume that is now lost. However, this second version is incomplete as well. Anne got no further than March 29, 1944, with her copying out and revision. The period from March 29 to August 1, 1944, again survives only in her day-to-day diary (version A), which she was still keeping.

She even drew up a list of pseudonyms for the book she was planning. At first she was going to call herself Anne Aulis. Then she crossed out the name Aulis and replaced it with Robin. Margot was to be Betty; her father, Otto, was to be Frederik; her mother, Edith, became Dora; Auguste and Hermann van Pels were Petronella and Hans van Daan; their son, Peter, was to be Alfred; and the last person to join them

20    in hiding, Fritz Pfeffer, was to be Albert Dussel. She also invented new names for the helpers. Bep Voskuijl was to become Elly Kuilmans; Miep was to be Anne van Santen; and her husband, Jan, was to be called Henk. Johannes Kleiman and Victor Kugler became Simon Koophuis and Harry Kraler.

In addition to the diary and the version on the loose sheets, Anne was also writing short stories and accounts of incidents in the Secret Annex during 1943 and 1944. An accounts book containing these stories has also been preserved.

Otto Frank now read all this, page after page, sheet after sheet. As he read, memories, images, and emotions must have come into his mind. Perhaps he compared his own memories with what his daughter had written, sometimes nodding, sometimes shaking his head. He must have been upset to realize how little he had known Anne—a realization all the harder to bear now that he had lost her forever and could not make up for it.

Did Anne, through her diaries, become a symbol of loss for Otto Frank—one in which his wife and Margot were included? Or did he begin to develop a rather guilty conscience about the other two, a sense of guilt when he thought about Anne, since from now on her diaries occupied such a large part of his life? I asked Fritzi Frank. She told me her husband had always thought it unfair that so much more attention was paid to Anne than to Margot; he would often say, "Margot was an angel."

Otto Frank must have suffered a great deal when he first read the diaries, and no doubt he also immediately realized, whether intuitively or consciously, that they were far superior to the usual kind of private diaries kept by teenage girls. He translated some passages into German to send to his relations

living in Switzerland: his mother, his sister, and her husband 21
and their two sons. However, these passages were not yet the
book *Het Achterhuis* that was to find such a huge response,
and still does. There was still another step to be taken.

Otto Frank took this step when he began typing out a transcript of his daughter's diaries, although he copied a selection
of entries rather than the whole text. He used the loose
sheets, Anne's version B, as the basis for his selection, but he
also chose entries or parts of entries that struck him as "the
essentials"[16] from the original diary, version A. He had only
version A available for the period after March 29, 1944, in any
case. In addition, he typed out some of the stories from the
accounts book.

There could have been several reasons Otto Frank did not
include all the entries in version B. Apart from a perhaps jus-
tified caution about the possibility of libel actions, the chief
among them were probably loyalty, a sense of justice, and a
certain squeamishness, typical of his generation, about the
candid description of a girl's physical development. He may
have omitted some of Anne's disparaging comments about her
mother out of loyalty to his dead wife, and certain dismissive
remarks about Mr. and Mrs. van Pels and Mr. Pfeffer from a
sense of fairness. Anne was constantly harping about the narrow outlook, rude behavior, ignorance, and so on of these
three in particular. Otto Frank was a grown man, and a man
of great discretion with a strong sense of justice. His view of
the people in hiding with him was naturally very different
from his teenage daughter's; he saw his companions in misfortune as individuals and was more tolerant in his view of
them. He must often have thought Anne's comments unjust,
thoughtless, or unreasonable, and omitted them for the sake

22    of objective truth. He may also have thought Anne's sometimes strikingly uninhibited accounts of her own physical
development were too private and intimate and so did not include them.

He probably thought his daughter's diaries were valuable
chiefly because they were a document of their times: the personal account of a Jewish girl in hiding in the Netherlands
during the German occupation. The "essentials" on which he
wanted to concentrate should therefore be as objective and
close to the facts as they could be, so it would be better for his
version of the diary to contain as few unjust and hurtful remarks as possible about people who could no longer defend
themselves (on the principle of *de mortuis nil nisi bonum*:
"speak nothing but good of the dead"). From this angle, his
decisions were entirely comprehensible and right.

However, he had left one important factor out of the equa-
tion. The diary of Anne Frank is not just a document of its
times, but a detailed account of a young girl's physical, intellectual, and spiritual growth into a woman under extraordinary circumstances, both external and internal, and amidst
extreme hardship and restrictions. Anne Frank describes a
real-life situation that we could hardly imagine without her
undoubtedly great talents, her honesty, her humor, and indeed her aggression. Unfair attacks on older people by the
young, which are natural and understandable even in normal
circumstances, can certainly be forgiven in conditions that
were anything but normal, and should not be censored out
of loyalty. A diary has to be written subjectively or it isn't
credible.

It isn't just Anne Frank's subjective approach, however, that
distinguishes her diary from many other diaries by girls of her

age, but the sometimes breathtaking objectivity with which she describes and comments on her companions in hiding and the situation in the Secret Annex with its unstable web of relationships. For instance, she was constantly thinking about the relationship with her mother that she found so difficult, relating it to other factors, seeking explanations and excuses, all with a detachment hard to imagine in a girl of her age.

But Otto Frank saw the diary more as a record of its time than as a young girl's personal and sometimes very intimate description of her own life, and consequently what he most wanted was for a large circle of friends to be able to read the "essentials" of his daughter's writings. That was why he made the transcript, which he then asked an acquaintance to look over and correct. A friend urged Otto Frank to publish the diary. However, it was not so easy to put this idea into practice, and for some time he could not find a publisher.

Only when a well-known historian, Jan Romein, published an article entitled "A Child's Voice"[17] did a publisher agree to issue the diary, as one in a series of books that were not to exceed a certain length. This meant that Otto Frank had to make further cuts in the text he had already abridged. Once again several passages were cut, some by Otto Frank himself, some by the publisher, who also deleted certain passages on Anne's sexuality and physical development. The book was published in the Netherlands by the firm Contact, Amsterdam, in the summer of 1947 under the title of *Het Achterhuis* (*The Annex*), with a subtitle reading *Diary Letters June 12, 1942–August 1, 1944*. Fifteen hundred copies of the first edition were printed. Anne Frank's wish to be a published writer had come true.

In 1950, when *Het Achterhuis* had already gone into its

24 sixth printing in the Netherlands, the first German edition appeared, published by the firm Lambert Schneider in Heidelberg under the title *Das Tagebuch der Anne Frank* and translated by Anneliese Schütz.

A new German translation was published in 1991, but the earlier version gave German readers their idea of Anne Frank for nearly forty years. Anneliese Schütz was a German journalist who, like the Franks, had fled to Amsterdam from the Nazi regime, and who made friends with them there. Apart from a few mistakes, her translation can be described as correct, but Anneliese Schütz was already quite elderly and could not echo Anne's youthful, fresh style, which was very close to spoken language, so in German the book sounded rather old-fashioned. Some of the subsequent attacks on the authenticity of the diaries (particularly frequent in Germany) may be put down to the style of this translation; its smooth, rather leisurely tone could be used to support the theory that the book had not really been written by a young girl.

There were also some changes of a "political" nature in Anneliese Schütz's translation. They had probably been made by agreement with Otto Frank: no doubt it was thought unwise to publish some of Anne Frank's anti-German remarks in a German edition. For example, in the entry of November 17, 1942, when Anne is listing the "rules and regulations" for the Secret Annex, she comes to the item: *Use of language: It is necessary to speak softly at all times. Only the language of civilized people may be spoken, thus no German.* The first German translation said only: *Languages: the language of civilized people . . . but softly!!!*

The first German edition of 4,500 copies was published, but it was not a great success at first. (Only when the paperback German edition was published in 1955 did sales gradually rise, particularly after the play by Albert Hackett and Frances Goodrich-Hackett was performed in many German cities and was very successful.) At about the same time, a French edition of the diary appeared, the *Journal de Anne Frank*, and in the United States and the United Kingdom *The Diary of a Young Girl* was published in 1952, in a translation by Mrs. B. M. Mooyart-Doubleday.

Today, according to information supplied by the Anne Frank Foundation in Basel, the diary of Anne Frank has appeared in more than fifty-five countries, has been translated into more than fifty-five languages, and has sold over 20 million copies.

And so another of Anne's wishes came true. She put it into words on April 5, 1944: *I don't want to have lived in vain like most people. I want to be useful or bring enjoyment to all people, even those I've never met. I want to go on living even after my death!*

She has lived on as almost no other girl, and no other writer, has done.

# 3 Anne Frank the Writer

## "I KNOW I CAN WRITE"

How can we get close to someone like Anne Frank after so many years—after a whole generation? If she had lived she would be entering her seventies now, and all the people who knew her, if they are still alive, are relatively old too. I cannot really go and ask them, "What was Anne like?" In fact, I don't want to ask them; I don't trust their memories. I know how unreliable memory can be.

I imagine one's memory of someone to be like a portrait sketched quickly and delicately in watercolors on a sheet of paper. Over the years the paper turns yellow and the colors fade. Every time someone asks for memories of that person the sheet of paper is brought out and, in attempting to convey an idea of the picture, contours are made bolder, a little color is dabbed on here and there, mistakes and misunderstandings are corrected. Perhaps, if there is a great deal of emotional involvement, the painting even spills over the edges of the outline. It happens so easily. What kind of person was Anne Frank? Cheerful? A dab of red. Sad? A blue shadow. Did people realize how special she was at the time? A strong black line is added to the contour. The picture changes with every question and every answer, until in the end you cannot make out the original delicate lines anymore, you scarcely recognize the faded colors, the hints, the guesses, the doubts; you cannot distinguish the point where truth and interpretation merge.

I have read all I could find about Anne Frank, including accounts by people who knew her or followed her trail, and I have spent a long time working on her diaries. Has it brought me any closer to her? Perhaps. But I don't want to rely too heavily on speculation. In what I say about her, I want to be guided mainly by what she wrote herself. The girl Anne is dead, but the writer Anne Frank will live on as long as she finds readers. I am therefore beginning Anne Frank's story with her work as a writer; here we have the diaries, the stories, all in black and white, although of course this is only one aspect of Anne as a person, only one piece of the truth.

What made this girl write? She wanted to keep a diary, but that is not unusual in adolescent girls, and teenagers of her time probably kept diaries more often than teenagers today. So there is nothing out of the ordinary about a girl sitting at a desk, leaning over the paper, blushing as she confides her secrets to her diary. However, it is obvious that Anne Frank wanted more than just a safe place for her secrets. She enjoyed writing for its own sake; it was a way to depict herself—a way to paint a verbal picture of herself and her place in the world.

An early example is the story of the essay Anne had to write as a punishment, set by a teacher because she had been talking in class. She describes it on Sunday, June 21, 1942, not long after beginning her diary.

28    *He assigned me extra homework. An essay on the subject "A*
*Chatterbox." A chatterbox, what can you write about that?*
*[. . .] I began thinking about the subject while chewing the tip*
*of my fountain pen. Anyone could ramble on and leave big*
*spaces between the words, but the trick was to come up with*
*convincing arguments to prove the necessity of talking. I*
*thought and thought, and suddenly I had an idea. I wrote the*
*three pages Mr. Keesing had assigned me and was satisfied. I*
*argued that talking is a female trait and that I would do my*
*best to keep it under control, but that I would never be able to*
*cure myself of the habit, since my mother talked as much as I*
*did, if not more, and that there's not much you can do about in-*
*herited traits.*

This little incident shows that Anne Frank enjoyed writing and found it a challenge. She tended to write well-rounded stories with a beginning, a middle, and an end, and it cannot be just because of her interesting situation that there are not many unfocused emotional outpourings in her diaries but a relatively large number of self-contained scenes where she shows her ability to confine herself to essential details. She never gave in to the obvious temptation for someone in her difficult position to write in an exaggerated way.

However, that still does not explain her growing passion for writing. Later on, it became almost an obsession. If she had simply liked narrative, writing for its own sake, she would have concentrated more on the stories she wrote for *Tales from the Secret Annex*. But even after August 1943, when she had begun writing stories and was feeling very enthusiastic about them, she did not neglect her diary. We cannot know how much she really wrote at this time, since version A, her original diary, is not preserved for the period between December 5, 1942, and December 22, 1943, but she did not abandon the diary in favor of the stories; in fact, the entries for 1944 are particularly long. Where did she get this passion for what is, after all, a very lonely pursuit?

The reason is fairly obvious: for her, writing was not lonely at all. Anne made her diary into a person; she made it "you," someone to talk to, "Kitty," the real friend she had wanted for so long. It was an extremely "literary" approach to adopt. Many children think up imaginary friends on whom they project their wishes and longings, but they do not very often make the imaginary friend into a literary character. However, this isn't exactly true. "Kitty" never really becomes a character in Anne Frank's writing. We hear hardly anything about her; instead, she enables Anne Frank to become a literary character herself. This shows that Anne could assess her gift even if her grasp of it may have been intuitive, for she always wrote best when she kept close to real life and the interpretation of real life. Her purely fictional stories are rather leisurely and wordy by comparison.

Her diary entry of June 20, 1942, in which she writes of her wish for a girlfriend and her decision to make the diary that friend, comes from version B, the one she was planning for publication; that is to say, it was really written not in 1942 but in the spring of 1944, by way of background information for her eventual readers. *Since no one would understand a word of my stories to Kitty if I were to plunge right in, I'd better provide a brief sketch of my life, much as I dislike doing so.* (There is no need for a background sketch of the writer's life in a private diary not intended for publication; at most the diarist may refer briefly to it.) In version B, Anne Frank explains why her diary entries take the form of letters: *To enhance the image of this long-awaited friend in my imagination, I don't want to jot down the facts in this diary the way most people would do, but I want the diary to be my friend, and I'm going to call this friend Kitty.*

In fact, the creation of Kitty took quite a long time. The entry for June 15, 1942, in version A of the diary contains considerably less on the subject of Anne's imaginary friend: *Jacqueline van Maarsen is supposedly my best friend, but I've never had a real friend.* Anne decided on the form her diary would take on September 21, 1942, when she says in version A (quoted here from the Critical Edition)*:

> *I would just love to correspond with somebody, so that is what I intend to do in future with my diary. I shall write it from now on in letter form, which actually comes to the same thing.*

> *Dear Jettje, (I shall simply say),*
> *My dear friend, both in future as well as now I shall have a lot to tell you. [. . .] Regards to everyone and kisses from*
> *Anne Frank*[18]

So at this point her correspondent is Jettje, not Kitty. However, the two names are connected because they come from the same book. Anne Frank twice mentions the children's writer Cissy van Marxveldt (1893–1948), who was extremely

---

*In quotations from version A taken from the Critical Edition, translations into other languages from Anne's Dutch to some extent reflect her occasionally faulty punctuation.

popular in the Netherlands at the time. On September 21, 1942, she notes: *Every other week Mr. Kleiman brings me a couple of books written for girls my age. I'm enthusiastic about the* Joop ter Heul *series. I've enjoyed all of Cissy van Marxveldt's books very much. I've read* The Zaniest Summer *four times, and the ludicrous situations still make me laugh.* And on October 14, 1942, she adds: *Cissy van Marxveldt is a terrific writer. I'm definitely going to let my own children read her books too.*

The *Joop ter Heul* series, named for its heroine, has five books in all. It follows the fortunes of a "club" of girls from school to marriage and motherhood. The subjects of the books are not very different from those of the girls' books published elsewhere in the world at the same time—stories with an almost educational feel to them, preparing girls for their future roles as wives and mothers. In style, however, they are quite different—more colloquial and amusing; it is tempting to say more modern. The first book in the series, although lightweight by today's standards, is particularly pleasant and easy to read, and we may safely assume that Cissy van Marxveldt had some influence on Anne Frank's own style. In any case, the names of the girls are interesting: Joop, Pop (Emilie), Phien (Philipiene), Marjan, Lou, Connie, Jettje, and—Kitty Francken. They are all members of the club and were Anne Frank's first correspondents.

Anne Frank wrote her first letter to the club on September 28, 1942. It is not important from a literary viewpoint, being almost a kind of "daydream" in which an adolescent girl identifies with characters from a book. However, I reproduce it here, although in abbreviated form (it can be found only in the Critical Edition, not in the Definitive Edition of the diary, and Anne did not incorporate it into version B).

32    *Sept. 28, 1942*

*To the whole club in general.*

*Dearest Kitty,*

When I am frightened at night, I get into Daddy's bed, he doesn't mind at all. One night the shooting went on so long that I bundled together all the bedthings and lay down on the floor next to his bed like a dog. 'Bye, Kitty Francken and friend François, from Anne Frank.

*Dearest Pop,*

When there is a storm or if I can't sleep, I can get in with Pim, he doesn't mind. Greetings to Kees ter Heul, 'bye, Pop, or Emilie ter Heul-Helmer, from Anne Frank.

*Dearest Phien,*

If I have to go to the w.c. at night, I wait till Daddy has to go too we often meet in the bathroom at night. Greetings to Bobbel Breed-Philipiene Breed-Greve, from Anne Frank.

She also addressed other members of the club in this letter. It is particularly interesting because it shows Anne Frank feeling so involved with the heroines of the books that she even sends greetings to their husbands or boyfriends. Elsewhere she writes to Emmy: *How are things with Janeau? Are you all right, you two, or do you still squabble every day and make up in the evenings, that is the best bit of all for sure.*[19] And on September 22, 1942, she writes to Kitty: *Dearest Kitty, Yesterday I wrote to Emmy and Jettje, but I prefer writing to you, you know that don't you and I hope the feeling is mutual.*[20]

She decided on Kitty as her correspondent, and her letters

to the others became less and less frequent; the last is dated November 13, 1942, and addressed to "Jetty." Anne Frank incorporated it into version B, dated November 12, 1942, but this time it is addressed to Kitty. Of course, we cannot know if there were any more letters to other members of the club. At some point, however, Anne Frank came to the decision to write only to Kitty, who had become *her* friend, and the other girls are not mentioned in version B. It may have been Kitty's similar last name, Francken, that made her Anne's choice. All Anne's longing for friendship and communication was now concentrated on Kitty.

However, even this original way of coping with her need for intimacy and company would not in itself make Anne Frank a writer. To be a writer, you must have the desire (and of course the ability) to portray yourself, giving form to your life, your ideas, and your needs, intensifying them so that you can put them down on paper. Anne Frank's mastery of that ability, despite her youth, must surely have been partly due to her situation. Her world had to be small enough to fit into the Secret Annex, its few rooms, the hallway, and the attic. The immediate surroundings of the Annex, which offered a little variety, at least at first, were confined to the firm's offices, and Anne could only occasionally look out at the world beyond through a crack in the curtains. The few people she saw through binoculars or walking along the street had to replace not only the whole city but also school, outings, trips, everything. Her only glimpse of natural beauty consisted of the leaves and flower spikes of the chestnut tree outside the window, a few clouds passing by, a seagull. She could make a forest out of a leaf, the whole wide world out of a drifting cloud. She created nature inside her head; a little moonlight now and then aroused her romantic feelings—and what really made her a writer was this ability to create wide-ranging emotions out of relatively small incidents and then describe them.

Equally important, however, was her wish to communicate with other people, people she did not know: this led to her decision to copy out her diary and adapt it for publication, which showed strong creative will. Anne Frank frequently read through and revised the second version of the diaries, and indeed the first. She corrected spelling mistakes, crossed out words and replaced them with others, and generally polished her writing. By the time she wrote the second version of her diary, Anne Frank was no longer just a young girl writing a diary, but a real writer with the clear intention of writing literature. We can get an idea of the extent of her concentration on literary form from the fact that she made more than 2,900 changes and corrections in all (taking the diaries and the loose sheets together). They included many corrections of spelling mistakes, but a number of changes to style and content as well. In a girl of her age, such concentrated revision shows not only creativity but also a good deal of objectivity and self-criticism.

It is pointless to wonder whether Anne would have become a writer if she could have lived her young life in normal circumstances, rather than in danger and in hiding. No one can say. Perhaps she would still have been a writer since she had abilities looking for expression, but the process would probably have taken longer. Perhaps she would not; she might have flung herself into life and all its pleasures instead of writing. As it was, however, while Anne the young girl had only a few square yards to live in, Anne the writer was embarking on the

great adventure of her life with a fountain pen and some
paper.

If I sound emotional here, it is because Anne Frank's story is so powerful. I have to be careful, though, not to idealize her too much or make her out to be very different from her many companions in misfortune. She was a writer but also a Jewish girl, one of many, and her existence and its extinction echoed those of other victims who never became famous. It is important to remember that she lived and died as one among millions of individuals; that must not be forgotten in our admiration for her diary.

# 4 The Story of the Frank Family

## "I LIVED IN FRANKFURT UNTIL I WAS FOUR"

Anne Frank's life, which was not to last even sixteen years, began in Frankfurt am Main, Germany, on June 12, 1929. Her life and above all her death were determined by her origins, for Anne Frank was Jewish.

Her family had close links with the city of Frankfurt. Their ancestors can be traced back as far as the Frankfurt ghetto* at the beginning of the sixteenth century.[21] Otto Frank, born in 1889, grew up in a prosperous middle-class family.

*Father was born in Frankfurt am Main to very wealthy parents: Michael Frank owned a bank and became a millionaire, and Alice Stern's parents were prominent and well-to-do. Michael Frank didn't start out rich; he was a self-made man. In his youth Father led the life of a rich man's son. Parties every week, balls, banquets, beautiful girls, waltzing, dinners, a huge house, etc. After Grandpa died, most of the money was lost, and after the Great War and inflation there was nothing left at all. (May 8, 1944)*

* Frankfurt ghetto: Frankfurt, like other European cities, once required Jews to live in a particular neighborhood, segregating them from the other city residents.

In fact, Michael Frank was not a millionaire but he was well-to-do—and liberal in his outlook. By far the majority of German Jews whose families had been in the country a long time (about 80 percent of them) were liberal rather than strictly orthodox in their religious views; they felt German and encouraged Jewish integration in all areas of life. This also explains why the Zionist movement in Germany found most of its supporters among the Orthodox Jews who had emigrated to the country from the east after the turn of the century.

It is obvious that the Frank family was liberal from the fact that neither Otto Frank nor his brothers and sister attended Jewish schools. Nor did the boys of the family celebrate their bar mitzvahs* on their thirteenth birthdays. Otto Frank went to the Lessing Grammar School, where he studied Latin and Greek but not Hebrew, which indeed he never learned. He grew up in Frankfurt, which had a higher proportion of Jewish citizens among its population as a whole than any other German city—sometimes as much as 10 percent. (The average Jewish population of Germany around 1900 was just under 1 percent.) A historical leaflet on Anne Frank published by the city of Frankfurt tells us that, "Around 1900 far more Jewish than Christian families could trace their ancestors in Frankfurt back to the late Middle Ages. They took as much pride in their roots as any of the 'genuine' citizens of Frankfurt, and indissolubly linked to that local and civic patriotism were a republican outlook, a broad-minded attitude, and tolerance."[22]

Otto Frank said later that he met with no anti-Semitism as a child. That is hard to believe, for although many Jews had

---

* Bar mitzvah: Hebrew, "son of commandment." A Jewish boy is regarded as reaching religious maturity at thirteen and goes through the bar mitzvah initiation ceremony.

roots in the city, even in Frankfurt there must have been signs of the anti-Semitism that had developed in Germany since 1870 and was now thought of in racial rather than religious terms. When Anne's father said he experienced no anti-Semitism, he probably meant it had never affected him personally. Like so many other Germans, Otto Frank served as a soldier on the Western Front in the First World War; he was decorated, and was an officer in the Reserve by the time he was demobilized. During the war his mother, Alice, sometimes did voluntary nursing work in a Frankfurt hospital.

Anne Frank was accurate in saying that the family had less money after her grandfather died, but that probably had less to do with his death (in 1908) than with economic conditions after the First World War. The family had of course made war loans, money lent to the government, which in itself meant financial losses when Germany lost the war. As a result of the war and restrictive currency regulations, the bank was doing badly. Otto Frank went to Amsterdam in the autumn of 1923 to found a branch there, but it had to be closed again a year later. (It was at this time that he met Johannes Kleiman, who was to play a large part in the Franks' story later when he helped them to hide.)

In 1925, at the age of thirty-six, Otto Frank married twenty-five-year-old Edith Holländer, daughter of a businessman whose family had lived in Aachen for a long time. Her father was co-owner of a wholesale metal firm dealing in the demolition and recycling of old iron. Margot was born on February 16, 1926. The family moved house that year, leaving the fashionable Westend district of Frankfurt for a new housing estate where not many Jews lived. They were still here at 307 Marbachweg when their second daughter, Annelies

Marie, known as Anne, was born on June 12, 1929. The atmosphere of Marbachweg has been described as liberal and progressive; the children of Protestant families played with the few Jewish and Catholic children. Anne joined this crowd of children. Margot already belonged to it.

The effects of the international economic crisis forced the Franks to move again in 1931, to a flat in Ganghoferstrasse. This was known as the "poets' quarter" of the city and was more like the Westend area, but the family's new home was smaller and cheaper than their old one. Their respectable bourgeois surroundings may have seemed to provide more protection from the National Socialists, who were becoming increasingly active and brutal. In March 1933, however, the Franks gave up this flat "as a result of changes in the economic situation"[23] and moved in with Anne's grandmother.

There were local elections in Frankfurt on March 12, 1933, and the Nazi party won forty-two of the eighty-five seats on the city council. The Jewish mayor, Ludwig Landmann, had resigned the day before. An appeal made by the Executive Committee of the Israelite Community in the community journal, and published the day before the Nazi boycott of April 1, 1933,* illustrates the situation of Jews at the time better than any explanations:

To members of the community:
In these difficult times we feel a strong need to address ourselves to our community. You may all be sure that we are doing our utmost, like other communities in Germany, to

---

* On April 1, 1933, the National Socialists organized a boycott of Jewish shops, legal offices, and medical practices throughout Germany. It was later known as the "April Boycott."

stand up for equal civic rights for German Jews, to support those in need and ensure the continued existence of our community.

Nothing can rob us of a thousand years of traditional links with our German homeland; no distress or danger can estrange us from the faith we have inherited from our fathers. We will stand up for ourselves with circumspection and with dignity.

If no one else will speak for us, then let the stones of this city speak on our behalf; it owes its prosperity in large part to Jewish achievements, and contains many institutions bearing witness to Jewish public spirit. Relations between the Jewish and non-Jewish citizens of Frankfurt have always been particularly close.

Do not lose heart! Close ranks! No honorable Jew should desert his post at this time. Help us to preserve our fathers' inheritance, and if the troubles of the times bear hard on individuals, then remember the words traditionally spoken at the coming Passover festival, the festival of our liberation: "They have risen up against us to destroy us from generation to generation, but the Holy One, praised be his name, has saved us out of their hand."

Frankfurt am Main, March 30, 1933; Executive
Committee of the Israelite Community.[24]

Reading this today, one could weep with rage as well as grief. The Executive Committee intended to stand up for equal civic rights and help the persecuted, maintaining links with its native land and its inherited faith. Then comes the appeal to honorable Jews not to "desert their posts" at this time. The choice of a military metaphor itself tells us much about the committee's attitude. These Jews thought and felt in such a very German way. Yet only a week later, on April 7, 1933, a new law was passed, defining "Jewish" for the first time as "non-German."[25]

The Executive Committee of the community was definitely not recommending emigration. Clearly, no one yet guessed or believed that the ultimate aim of the National Socialists would be to rid Germany of all Jews (although Hitler's *Mein Kampf*, which made his intentions clear, had been published in 1925–26).

Even so, the Franks were thinking of emigrating. Here they differed from many other Jews who were biding their time, hoping the Nazi persecution would pass. But emigrating with two small children was not a decision to be taken lightly; what would the family live on?

Four years earlier, Otto Frank's brother-in-law Erich Elias had emigrated with his own family to Basel in Switzerland, where he was now working as a representative for the firm of Opekta. He arranged for Otto Frank to be offered a job building up a Dutch agency for Opekta in Amsterdam. This business opportunity, and the fact that Otto Frank already knew Amsterdam from the time of his failed banking venture and had friends there, probably led him to decide to emigrate to Amsterdam.

At any rate, Otto Frank went to the Netherlands in the summer of 1933, and in September an interim entry was made in the Amsterdam commercial register for the firm of Dutch Opekta Ltd.* The business of the company is given as "Trading in pectin."

* The firm of Opekta made pectin—a jelling agent still used in jam-making today. Opekta is also still in existence.

Anne's mother, Edith Frank, was waiting in Aachen with Margot and Anne. She soon followed her husband, and shortly afterward Margot joined them in their new home at No. 37 Merwedeplein. Four-year-old Anne arrived in February and was "put on the table as a birthday present for Margot." Her grandmother Alice moved to Basel, where her daughter and son-in-law were already living, and Otto Frank's two brothers emigrated, one to London and one to Paris. This was the end of the Frank family's centuries-old connection with the city of Frankfurt. But it was not the end of their connection with German history and the history of the Third Reich.

# 5 The Netherlands and the Jews

**"THE DUTCH AREN'T TO BLAME BECAUSE WE JEWS ARE SO BADLY OFF"**

Amsterdam, like Frankfurt, was an old international center of banking and trade, and the diamond industry was particularly prominent. Again like Frankfurt, Amsterdam had a relatively high proportion of Jews, about one-tenth of the whole population, but in contrast to Frankfurt and other German cities it had never had a Jewish ghetto.

The first mention of Jews in what is now the state of the Netherlands was in 1295, in a pastoral letter.[26] Like the Jews of other Christian countries, these people probably lived chiefly by trade and financial dealings, since Jews were not allowed to learn crafts and join the craft guilds. However, there were probably not very many of them, even when Jewish refugees from the Inquisition in sixteenth-century Spain and Portugal settled in the Netherlands.

Only when Amsterdam became an international trading center in the seventeenth century did more and more Jewish people arrive in the Netherlands. In 1616 an Amsterdam rabbi mentioned in a letter that the inhabitants of the city would like its population to expand and were ready to pass laws and decrees allowing everyone religious freedom. All

44   could live according to their faith, so long as they did not make it publicly obvious that their religion was not that of most citizens of Amsterdam. Many Marranos,* Jews from Spain and Portugal, had settled in the city and gone back to practicing the Jewish faith; other Jews had followed them, said the rabbi, and had built a small synagogue where they met unobtrusively.

In reality, the people of Amsterdam were probably not quite so generous and tolerant, for Amsterdam was a Reformed† city where the practice of Catholicism was forbidden. However, foreigners and those of other faiths were never expelled. A decree of 1616 mentions only three strict rules of conduct for Jews: they are forbidden to revile Christianity in speech or writing; they are forbidden to convert a Christian to Judaism; and they are forbidden to have sexual intercourse with Christian women (including prostitutes).[27]

These were relatively mild restrictions by comparison with all the pogroms (massacres) in other countries. However, Jews could not have been said to enjoy the same civic rights as Christians, even if they were protected from real persecution. They could not, for instance, join a guild (although there were exceptions in Amsterdam for printers and also, with some restrictions, surgeons, apothecaries, and brokers).

In the second half of the seventeenth century the number

* The term used for Jews of Spain and Portugal forcibly baptized under the Inquisition, who secretly still practiced their Jewish faith and were finally expelled at the end of the fifteenth century. Large "Portuguese communities" formed in Amsterdam, Hamburg, and London.
† Reformed Protestants were followers of Calvin (1509–64), a French Swiss reformer whose doctrines had followers in large areas of Western Europe (France, Scotland, and the Netherlands).

of poorer Ashkenazi Jews*, Jews of Central and Eastern Europe, increased in the city. They were not economically well
off and were regarded as foreigners, but the authorities gave
them a certain amount of protection and they finally achieved
equal civic rights in 1848. After the establishment of the diamond industry, Amsterdam developed a large Jewish working
class with its own trade unions, in contrast to Germany.

The existing religious tolerance was probably one of the
reasons Jewish assimilation into the rest of the population
and the holding of "liberal" views were not very important
in Amsterdam until the 1920s. The Jews of the Netherlands
were spared pogroms until the German occupation. To say
the Dutch were fundamentally well disposed to Jews would
be going too far, but unlike the Germans they were willing to
"live and let live."

The Dutch law of 1849 relating to foreigners stated that "all
foreigners who can support themselves adequately, either fi-
nancially or by their own efforts, [. . .] may be allowed entry
into the Netherlands."[28]

About thirty thousand Jews emigrated from Germany and
Austria to the Netherlands between 1933 and 1938. In relation to the population as a whole and the size of its territory,
the Netherlands took in more refugees from Nazi Germany
and Austria than any other country. However, there were Fas-
cist tendencies even in the Netherlands, as in all European

---

* Ashkenazi Jews: Hebrew, *ashkenazim*, in the Old Testament; members of a people
living in the north of Palestine. The concept was transferred to the Jews of Central
and Eastern Europe (named after the usual word for Germany among Jews after the
Middle Ages, Ashkenaz). Their everyday language was Yiddish. The Jews from the
Iberian peninsula were Sephardim.

**46**   countries. The National-Socialistische Beweging (NSB) was
founded in 1931 on the model of the German National So-
cialist Party, under the leadership of an engineer called Anton
Mussert, but it never attracted mass support—not even later,
under German occupation.

After the National Socialists had won the German elections, the Netherlands still maintained the policy of strict
neutrality that had served them well in the First World War,
but after the Anschluss (the union of Germany and Austria),
the Dutch government's attitude toward German and Austrian
Jews became increasingly harsh. In view of all the applica-
tions for immigration being received from foreign Jews, they
feared there would be too many foreigners in the country, and
of course they did not want to annoy their powerful neighbors to the east. Any foreigners still allowed into the Netherlands had almost no rights and could not get work permits. A
decree issued by Justice Minister Goseling in 1938 stated that
refugees from Germany and Austria were to be regarded as
"undesirable aliens." They were allowed to stay only if they
could prove they were in danger of death in Germany, and the
threat of a German concentration camp was not accepted
as an argument. (How strongly laws on alien immigrants re-
semble each other in "civilized" countries—unless, of course,
those aliens are useful and desirable as "guest workers.")

After the violence of Crystal Night,* Justice Minister Goseling allowed eight thousand refugees into the Netherlands

---

\* Crystal Night, or *Kristallnacht:* the night of November 9, 1938, so called because of
the broken glass from all the windows smashed during the Nazi pogrom, or mas-
sacre, carried out that night. Ninety-one Jews were murdered, and almost all the synagogues in the German Reich were destroyed or badly damaged, as well as more than
seven thousand Jewish shops.

(some forty to fifty thousand had applied), but he insisted that 47
Jewish organizations should build and pay for a refugee camp.
This was the Westerbork camp later used by the Germans as a
transit camp for the deportation of Jews, in particular those
destined for the concentration camps of Auschwitz and Sobibor. (Justice Minister Goseling himself was taken to Buchenwald concentration camp as a hostage after the Germans
invaded the Netherlands, and "perished" there soon afterward.)

On May 10, 1940, German troops attacked the Netherlands, and the dream of neutrality was over. The Dutch army
could not stand up to the invaders. After the center of Rotter-
dam was bombed on May 14, the Netherlands surrendered,
and the royal family went into exile in London. As a "Ger-
manic brother state" the Netherlands was not placed under a
military government but had a German administration imposed under Reich Commissar Seyss-Inquart. Within a short
time the Jews were being persecuted here too. First kosher*
slaughter was forbidden, then all non-Dutch Jews had to
leave the coastal areas, and soon afterward Jewish shops were
seized and all Jews registered.

Resistance groups formed among the Dutch population in
the first weeks and months of the occupation, and soon there
were many clashes between the paramilitary section of the
NSB and the people in the Jewish quarter of Amsterdam.
When an NSB member was injured during riots in February
and died, the SS leader and police chief Hans Rauter had four
hundred Jews between the ages of twenty and thirty-five arrested in a raid; they were taken to Mauthausen and killed.
On February 25, 1941, there was a general strike of workers

* Kosher: Hebrew, "fit, proper," relating to the commands of Jewish religious law, especially about the ritual slaughter of beasts appropriate for eating.

**48**     in Amsterdam, Hilversum, and Zaandam—an act of protest
unique in Europe. On this occasion a famous saying was
coined: "Those dirty *moffen** had better keep their dirty paws
off our dirty Jews!"[29] (A remark that is nothing if not ambiva-
lent!) The strike was broken after three days, and in March
the first public executions of Dutch citizens were carried out
as a deterrent.

The "Aryanization of Jewish shops and businesses" began
in March 1941, with the aim of removing Jewish elements
from the economy. It ended a year later with the confiscation
of all Jewish property. As in Germany, Jews were subject to
special laws and dismissed from any public services. Decree
followed decree. All Dutch Jews must hand in their radio sets.
Jewish children must go to Jewish schools. Jews could not
visit public libraries anymore, could not walk in the park anymore, or go to the swimming pool, and so on. Notices went
up everywhere saying "Jews Forbidden." Jews could not move
house or travel without a permit. Jews could not employ non-
Jewish domestic servants. They could not drive cars. All Jews
over the age of six had to display the Star of David† promi-
nently on their clothing. Jews could not travel by train anymore, even with German permission. Jews could not buy
anything in non-Jewish shops or pursue any athletic activities
in public. Jews could not leave home between eight in the
evening and six in the morning.

The Germans were introducing into the Netherlands and
other occupied countries the measures they had already put

---

*Mof*, pl. *moffen:* Dutch term of abuse for the Germans, especially in the Second
World War.
† A yellow star with a black border, with the word "Jew" in the middle in letters that,
contemptuously, imitated Hebrew script.

into practice at home. First came the removal of Jews from public services and their registration, then their concentration into ghettolike areas, and finally their physical extermination.

When the first anti-Jewish laws were passed in the Netherlands, those Jews who had fled from Germany must have known what was happening, even if the restrictions were imposed separately rather than all at once. A carefully judged series of prohibitions was part of the plan; it undermined the will of the victims to resist, and not just among the non-Jewish population. You couldn't travel by tram anymore? Well, you could put up with that. You couldn't sit on a park bench anymore? A pity, but it was bearable. You couldn't go to the swimming pool? Well, it didn't often get so hot in the Netherlands as to be really unpleasant. People got used to the restrictions, managed somehow or other, sent their children to Jewish schools when they were told to do so, observed the curfew. What else could they do?

The non-Jewish population suffered during the occupation too, and hatred for the German occupying powers increased. However, opposition was not universal among the Dutch and the dividing line between good and bad, friend and foe, often ran right through families. Some thirty thousand Dutchmen applied to join the Waffen-SS* when the Germans were recruiting volunteers for the Eastern Front, and seventeen thousand were enlisted. Only in the course of 1942 did an organized resistance movement gradually form.

The Jews had been forced to found a Jewish Council; its main function after January 1942 was to organize the transport of Jews to one of the assembly camps, of which Wester-

---

* The armed branch of the SS.

50    bork was the largest. The Jewish Council was told it must fill
the requisite transport quotas for Westerbork, and if the figures were not right there would be punitive raids.

When it was made compulsory to wear the Star of David,
many Jews tried to go into hiding with Dutch friends. More
than twenty-five thousand are thought to have made the attempt, and roughly eight to nine thousand of these fell into
German hands. The numbers have not been established with
any certainty; according to other statistics there were twenty-
eight thousand in hiding, eighteen thousand of whom are said
to have avoided discovery. Whichever figure is right, it is still
astonishing that so many Dutch people were ready to offer
help, for the Germans had threatened anyone who hid Jews
or helped them to hide with deportation to a concentration
camp. (The Dutch who helped Jews did not always act out of
pure kindness. Sometimes rich Jews paid a lot of money for
help. Hatred for the German occupying power may have been
the main motive on other occasions.)

The various resistance groups also tried to find hiding
places for Jews and put them in touch with potential helpers,
particularly when the Center for Jewish Emigration began sending out call-up notices. This "authority" had been
founded by the Gestapo* in the spring of 1941. Its chief pur-
pose was to send out such call-up notices, allegedly for work
in the east, but really for deportation to Auschwitz and Sobibor. (Later on, babies and old people were "called up" too.)

When a call-up notice came for Margot on July 5, 1942, the
Franks knew it was time to go underground, and they went to
the hiding place they had already prepared.

---

* Gestapo: short for *Geheimes Staatspolizei*, the secret police of the Third Reich.

# Before Going into Hiding

## "A HEAVENLY EXISTENCE"

We know what happened to Anne Frank between her arrival in Amsterdam and the time when the family went into hiding partly from her own reminiscences in her diary and book of stories, partly from the memories of Miep Gies, and also from interviews in 1987–88 by the Dutch documentary filmmaker Willy Lindwer with Hannah Pick-Goslar, a friend of Anne who features as Hanneli Goslar in the actual diary and under the pseudonym of Lies Goosens in the first edition of *The Diary of a Young Girl*.[30]

Anne arrived in Amsterdam and the flat at 37 Merwedeplein in February 1934. A good deal of building work was going on in the south of Amsterdam at the time, and many Jews who had escaped from the Nazis settled there. Miep Gies tells us there was a saying in Amsterdam that on the No. 8 tram "the ticket taker *also* spoke Dutch."[31]

The children, Anne and Margot, settled in well and soon learned Dutch—much more quickly than their mother did. Anne made friends with Hanneli Goslar, only a few months older than herself, who had escaped from Berlin with her parents and who also lived in Merwedeplein, at No. 31. The two

52    girls met soon after Hanneli's arrival and became close friends. Their parents made friends as well, although unlike the Franks the Goslars were very devout and kept the religious laws that determine the whole way of life of Orthodox Jews.

The two girls also both went to the Montessori kindergarten not far from Merwedeplein. After leaving this kindergarten they both went to the sixth public Montessori school—today called the Anne Frank School. They had to leave in the autumn of 1941 because of the anti-Jewish laws and transfer to the newly founded Jewish Lyceum. Although Anne and Hanneli were close friends, they did not spend all their free time together. As the daughter of a devout Orthodox family, Hanneli was not allowed to go to school on the Sabbath (Saturday). She also learned Hebrew and had religious education lessons on Sunday morning and on Wednesdays (when most children had the afternoon off school). Anne, on the other hand, went to school like other children on Saturday and did not learn Hebrew. In the interview with Willy Lindwer, Hanneli talked about their games together and how they particularly liked going to Otto Frank's office with him on a Sunday and playing there, especially with the telephones. There was a phone in each room, so they kept ringing each other up. They also played games like hopscotch in the street, or tipped water out of the windows on people walking past below.

There were really three friends, Anne, Hanneli, and Sanne, but Sanne went to a different school and had a close friend there too, as Anne records in her diary. Hanneli Goslar describes them as perfectly normal girls who sometimes quarreled but always made up again.

Anne collected photos of movie stars; Hanneli was not par-

ticularly interested in that, but they both collected photos of
the children of the Dutch and English royal families. (This
may have been the beginning of Anne's later passion for the
family trees of the European royal houses.) In October 1940
Hanneli had a little sister. Margot and Anne visited her every
Sunday to watch as the baby was fed and bathed.

Hanneli also recalls that Anne was always playing with her
long, dark hair, and that she had a physical peculiarity: she
could dislocate her shoulders whenever she liked and
thought it was funny to make all the other children laugh
with this trick.

She was very pretty, says Hanneli, always at the center of
attention at school, and she liked it when boys looked at
her. "She liked being important—that isn't a bad quality. I remember that my mother, who liked her very much, used to
say, 'God knows everything, but Anne knows everything
better.' "[32]

There was a rift in the friendship between Hanneli Goslar
and Anne when Hanneli made friends with another girl from
a devout Jewish family and used to play with her on Sabbath
after synagogue. Much later, on November 27, 1943, Anne
dreamed about Hanneli and wrote in her diary: *Last night, just
as I was falling asleep, Hanneli suddenly appeared before me.
[. . .] I saw Hanneli, and no one else, and I understood why. I
misjudged her, wasn't mature enough to understand how difficult
it was for her. She was devoted to her girlfriend, and it must have
seemed as though I were trying to take her away. The poor thing,
she must have felt awful!*

What did Anne look like? There are many photographs of
her; her father liked taking pictures, and later, after the
Franks and their friends in hiding were arrested, Miep Gies

salvaged some of the family photo albums as well as Anne's diaries. Miep describes her as a delicate, attractive child and that is what the photographs show, but she seems always to have been slightly overshadowed by her prettier sister. Miep describes an invitation to the Franks:

"We were seated at the table, and Margot and Anne were called. Anne ran in. She was now eight years old, still somewhat thin and delicate, but with electric gray-green eyes with green flecks. Her eyes were very deeply set, so that when they were half-closed, they appeared to be shrouded in dark shade. Anne had her mother's nose and her father's mouth, but with a slight overbite and cleft chin.

"We were meeting Margot for the first time. [. . .] Margot was ten years old, very pretty, also with shiny dark hair. Both girls had their hair cut just below their ears, parted on the side, held back by a barrette. Margot's eyes were dark. She was shy and quiet with us, and very, very well mannered, as was little Anne. Margot's smile made her face even prettier."[33]

And how did Anne see herself? On the second page of her diary, one of those probably left blank at first, she added this description when the family had gone into hiding. (This entry is from the Critical Edition and is not in the Definitive Edition of the diary):

> *The 7 or 12 beautiful features (not mine mind you!) should come here, then I can fill in which ones I have, and which ones I don't.*
> *28 Sept. 1942 (drawn up by myself.)*
> 1. *blue eyes, black hair (no.)*
> 2. *dimples in cheeks (yes.)*
> 3. *dimple in chin (yes.)*

4. *widow's peak (no.)*
5. *white skin (yes.)*
6. *straight teeth (no.)*
7. *small mouth (no.)*
8. *curly eyelashes (no.)*
9. *straight nose (yes.) (at least so far.)*
10. *nice clothes (sometimes.) (not nearly enough in my opinion.)*
11. *nice fingernails (sometimes.)*
12. *intelligent (sometimes.)*[34]

Anne was very sociable, says Miep, and liked autograph albums, secrets, and chattering. She was inquisitive and talkative, always asking questions and talking about her girl-friends. In general she got good grades at school except in math. She was a quick learner but, Miep says, "was turning into a social butterfly."[35] Margot, on the other hand, was do-ing very well at school, where she was an outstanding student who enjoyed class and always got good grades. A teacher who knew both girls said later that she would have thought Mar-got was the one more likely to have written an interesting di-ary. (As we know from Anne, Margot did in fact keep a diary, but hers was lost.)

Miep tells us that Anne loved going to the movies. She kept up her interest in films and film stars even in the Secret An-nex, and writes in her diary about the photos she put up in her room, the magazine *Cinema & Theatre* that Mr. Kugler brought her every Monday, and how her mother said Anne would never need to go to the movies later because she had the plots, the casts, and the reviews of all the films inside her head already.

Anne obviously enjoyed acting a part in front of an audience. Miep Gies writes: "Anne had developed the skill of mimicry. She would mimic anyone and anything, and very well at that: the cat's meow, her friend's voice, her teacher's authoritative tone. We couldn't help laughing at her little performances, she was so skilled with her voice. Anne loved having an attentive audience, and loved to hear us respond to her skits and clowning."[36]

When the Germans occupied the Netherlands in May 1940, Anne was just under eleven; when she went into hiding, she was exactly thirteen years old. In those two years a great deal had changed in her life. The major change was probably when she had to leave the Montessori School in September 1941 and transfer to the Jewish Lyceum. And there was another good-bye to be said during those years—one of special personal importance to her: her grandmother from Aachen, who had been living with the Franks since 1938, died in January 1942. Anne had been very fond of her and mentions her several times in her diary.

Otherwise Anne's life pursued its usual unclouded course, as she describes it herself, looking back later in the entry of March 7, 1944:

*When I think back to my life in 1942, it all seems so unreal. The Anne Frank who enjoyed that heavenly existence was completely different from the one who has grown wise within these walls. Yes, it was heavenly. Five admirers on every street corner, twenty or so friends, the favorite of most of my teachers, spoiled rotten by Father and Mother, bags full of candy and a big allowance. What more could anyone ask for? [. . .] The teachers were amused and entertained by my clever an-*

swers, my witty remarks, my smiling face and my critical mind. That's all I was: a terrible flirt, coquettish and amusing. I had a few plus points, which kept me in everybody's good graces: I was hardworking, honest and generous. I would never have refused anyone who wanted to peek at my answers, I was magnanimous with my candy, and I wasn't stuck-up [. . .] I look back at that Anne Frank as a pleasant, amusing, but superficial girl, who has nothing to do with me.

This self-assessment, harsh as it may seem, is probably quite close to the truth, although it is hard to imagine any children—and more particularly Jewish children—being able to lead a relatively carefree life during those years. Her parents probably tried to ensure that their two daughters grew up with as few anxieties as possible, not wanting them to understand how hard things were for adults. It is interesting to notice Anne's detached account of the anti-Jewish laws in her diary, where she lists them without adding personal comments. There is no rage or anger or despair—not even a slight regret over all she has to give up. Her one comment is: *Jacque* [her friend Jacqueline Sanders] *always said to me, "I don't dare do anything anymore, 'cause I'm afraid it's not allowed."* (June 20, 1942)

Only on June 24, 1942, does she complain, once, of having to walk to the dentist's on a very hot day during school lunchtime because Jews were no longer allowed to travel by tram. In the same entry Anne mentions that her father has taken her mother's bicycle to a friendly Christian family for safekeeping. However, both these details are from version B, which she wrote only in 1944; that is, when the full gravity of the situation had become clear to her in retrospect.

58     In the original version of her diary, from the time when she began keeping it until she went into hiding, she writes only about her birthday presents, her various girlfriends, her "admirer" Hello Silberberg, and Peter Schiff, her childhood sweetheart, whom she plans to marry one day. She describes her birthday party, when a Rin Tin Tin film was shown, and a Ping-Pong club she and some other girls started. She also writes at length and with rather merciless precision about the other pupils at her school, both boys and girls. She makes only very brief references to her own life, her birth in Frankfurt, her stay in Aachen, and the move to Amsterdam; and the same applies to her kindergarten, the Montessori School, and her grandmother's death. She sticks pictures of her grandmother and Margot in the diary, both taken on the beach, and adds a letter from her father written three years before. She describes going to an ice-cream parlor, and how Jacque slept over with the Franks. And she gives a detailed account of a conversation with Hello, whose grandparents think Anne is still too young for him. Everything else, all references to the oppressive situation under the anti-Jewish laws, are from version B, including the remark that Oasis or Delphi is *the nearest ice-cream parlor that allows Jews.*

Obviously Anne Frank had no idea that for the last year her parents had been getting ready to go into hiding. Even the conversation with her father in which he prepared her for the forthcoming move is something added afterward, perhaps for literary reasons, to warn of coming events and heighten suspense. Anne did not know that the whole family was about to move to a hiding place until the call-up notice came for Margot, only a day before they went.

*The door was locked and no one was allowed to come into our* 59
*house any more. Daddy and Mummy had long ago taken mea-*
*sures, and Mummy assured me that Margot would not have to*
*go and that all of us would be leaving next day. Of course I*
*started to cry terribly and there was an awful to-do in our*
*house. Daddy and Mummy had taken a whole lot of things out*
*of the house already, but when it comes to the point one is*
*bound to miss so much.*[37]

She was certainly alarmed, and "of course" began to cry, but
she accepted the idea of going into hiding without protest.
The phrase "but when it comes to the point one is bound to
miss so much" sounds like an echo of something said by the
adults. Anne herself is unlikely to have invented it.

Later, in version B, she tells us what she packed in her
school bag: *The first thing I stuck in was this diary, and then
curlers, handkerchiefs, schoolbooks, a comb and some old letters.
Preoccupied by the thought of going into hiding, I stuck the cra-
ziest things in the bag, but I'm not sorry. Memories mean more to
me than dresses.*

Alarmed as she must have been, she says nothing about any
fears, only her sorrow at having to leave Moortje, her beloved
cat, behind. If the experience of going into hiding was not
really a severe shock to her, and did not become a destructive
trauma, it was probably mainly because of her love of adventure and the pleasure she took in excitement and change.
That was surely not entirely due to her youth.

# 7 The Secret Annex

## "WE ARE ALL ALIVE, BUT WE DON'T KNOW WHY OR WHAT FOR"

What kind of hiding place did Anne now move into, more or less aware that she might not be able to leave it again for a very, very long time? At least she could still be with her family: in this she was very fortunate, as parents and children were usually parted from each other when they went into hiding. And the hiding place was not a poky hole, attic, or cellar, but part of a real house, and was even half familiar to Anne already. It was at 263 Prinsengracht, in the same building as the offices occupied since December 1940 by her father's company—a tall, narrow red brick building like many in the area.

There were three doors at the front of the building, looking out on the canal. One led up a steep flight of stairs to the attic, one straight to the storerooms, and the official front door led up a few steps to a landing with two doors opening from it. One of these doors led to the large, light office where Miep, Bep, and Mr. Kleiman worked. The second opened into a corridor with a door to the *small, dark, stuffy back office. This used to be shared by Mr. Kugler and Mr. van Daan, but now Mr. Kugler is its only occupant.* At the end of the passage there were a few more steps and then you reached Otto Frank's private office, described by Anne as *the showpiece of the entire building. Elegant mahogany furniture, a linoleum floor covered with throw rugs, a radio, a fancy lamp, everything first class.* There was a large kitchen next to this office. From the downstairs passage, a simple wooden staircase led up to a landing with two doors; the left-hand door gave access to the front of the building, containing the storerooms and the stairs to the attic, and the right-hand door was the way to the real hiding place, the Secret Annex at the back of the building. A little later this door was disguised by a movable bookcase.

*No one would ever suspect there were so many rooms behind that plain gray door. There's just one small step in front of the door, and then you're inside. Straight ahead of you is a steep flight of stairs. To the left is a narrow hallway opening onto a room that serves as the Frank family's living room and bedroom. Next door is a smaller room, the bedroom and study of the two young ladies of the family. To the right of the stairs is a windowless washroom with a sink. The door in the corner leads to the toilet and another one to Margot's and my room. If you go up the stairs and open the door at the top, you're surprised to see such a large, light and spacious room in an old canalside house like this. It contains a stove (thanks to the fact that it used to be Mr. Kugler's laboratory) and a sink. This will be the kitchen and bedroom of Mr. and Mrs. van Daan, as well as the general living room, dining room and study for us all. A tiny side room is to be Peter van Daan's bedroom. Then, just as in the front part of the building, there's an attic and a loft. So there you are. Now I've introduced you to the whole of our lovely Annex!* (July 9, 1942)

62   Today 263 Prinsengracht is a museum. The offices of the Anne Frank organization and the exhibition rooms occupy the front of the building. The Secret Annex, however, has been restored and is in very much the same state as it was when Anne lived there. Groups of visitors now constantly flock in to look around.

I imagine myself sitting on the sofa in the room that Anne shared first with Margot, then with the dentist Fritz Pfeffer. It is a small room; it would be small even for just one person. Daylight comes in through the window—but no, of course the window was kept covered when the Franks were in hiding. On the very first day they made curtains which, as Anne wrote, did not really deserve the name, *since they're nothing but scraps of fabric, varying greatly in shape, quality and pattern, which Father and I stitched crookedly together with unskilled fingers.* A small, cramped room would seem smaller and more cramped than ever with its only window curtained both day and night. I think how eagerly I pull back my own curtains in the morning.

There are still pictures of film stars stuck to the wall over the sofa bed. The sofa on which Anne slept is not very long. At first it may have been long enough; later it was extended with the help of chairs. The same chairs into which Mr. Pfeffer bumped in the morning when he was doing his limbering-up exercises. They shifted back and forth under Anne's sleepy head while he exercised to keep fit and then dressed. And there is the little table; Anne had to compete with him for it. A tiny room, far too small for two people to live and sleep in when they were as unlike each other in every way as Anne Frank and Fritz Pfeffer.

How could it have worked anyway? Eight people so different in age, background, and character, shut up together for more than two years in a space amounting to about five hundred and fifty square feet. How did they manage to work out the everyday routine that was so essential, the sense of normality more urgently needed than ever in such an extreme situation?

Human beings can probably create a sense of everyday life anywhere. Everyday life is natural; it is made up of routine actions that are done without question and require no particular psychological adjustment. The greater the tension or danger confronting us, the more important it is to find support and relief in everyday life.

A sense of normality was created surprisingly fast by the eight people in hiding, even though they were called upon to adjust drastically—we have only to think of the sudden change from the Franks' big flat and their freedom of movement to a cramped, confined environment. But since they already knew the building and their helpers, and therefore had comparatively few new impressions to absorb, they managed to make things seem normal relatively quickly. The time factor was probably the most difficult change to adjust to, now that they could no longer pass the time as usual. Once in hiding they had to find other ways of spending their days, other occupations, other interests. It was difficult, and they were not always successful, nor were they all successful to the same extent. On December 13, 1942, Anne Frank wrote in her diary: *Our thoughts are subject to as little change as we are. They're like a merry-go-round, turning from the Jews to food, from food to politics.* But you can get used to anything. Squabbling and the struggle against boredom are major factors for people living at close quarters.

64    I have only two documents to help me describe the individual people who lived in the Secret Annex and their relationships with each other: Anne's diary and Miep Gies's book, *Anne Frank Remembered.* Both are very personal accounts—and thus inevitably biased and certainly incomplete. However, I will make the attempt.

# 8 Mr. and Mrs. Frank

## "I KNOW I'M AN INDEPENDENT PERSON"

Without doubt, Otto Frank was the central figure in organizing life for those eight people in a very small space and under extremely difficult circumstances.

Miep Gies describes him as a tall, thin, very cultivated but rather nervous man. During the extremely difficult period the eight Jews spent in hiding, however, he developed extraordinary intellectual and spiritual resources. He was in charge, conciliating and soothing the others, making efforts to understand them all. He was "the calm one, [. . .] the one who balanced everyone out. He was the leader, the one in charge."[38] He made all the decisions affecting the group as a whole, showing not only his great competence but extraordinary self-restraint. This was probably what Anne meant when she wrote on September 28, 1942, of *Pim's extreme diffidence.*

This kind of self-control, almost amounting to self-sacrifice, is a quality I have often found in people of Otto Frank's age and social class. A willingness to put the task in hand first and yourself last derives from the nineteenth-century ethic of responsibility, often called the Protestant ethic. Perhaps this is the positive side of an education teaching the virtues of discipline and duty; the negative side is subservience and blind obedience.

Otto Frank accepted responsibility as something quite natural; none of the others could have done the job, but he probably did not want it much.

He had already shown great foresight on several occasions. He had emigrated as early as 1933, he had "Aryanized" his own company, and with Kleiman's help he had prepared the hiding place, stocking it with furniture, household linen, and food. He was certainly aware before the others of the difficulties that might arise, living at such close quarters. The main problem was how to devise some form of normal everyday life acceptable to them all, so that they could at least construct a fairly stable network of relationships and prevent chaos from breaking out whenever there was the slightest tension. If that was to be done, time must be given a structure; each of the inhabitants of the Secret Annex must be provided with set routines.

This was no simple task, particularly where Anne, Margot, and Peter were concerned. Here were three young people who would be spending weeks and months without anything to relieve the monotony of their lives, unable to take any physical exercise to speak of and, above all, without the normal daily routine of going to school and doing household tasks. And there was no end in sight. I have tried imagining just six weeks of summer holidays spent in a small flat with my three young daughters, unable to go out or do anything, and I just can't think what it would be like. On average, few people can sleep for more than eight hours a night, so even allowing three hours for personal hygiene and eating meals, that still leaves thirteen hours to fill: thirteen hours, day after day.

Otto Frank had anticipated these problems. On July 11, 1942, Anne notes that she doubts if they will be bored for the time being. They had plenty to read, she said, and were going to buy a lot of games. Later on, however, it seems that they did not play games very often. Otto Frank soon made sure they were all following an intensive course of study as well as doing the necessary household tasks. This would have reflected his own interests, but it also suited his daughters, who were eager to learn. He kept them at work even on the subjects they disliked (Anne, for instance, hated math) and ordered a shorthand correspondence course, through the helpers, for all three young people: Margot, Anne, and Peter. Later, he also ordered a Latin course for Margot and himself. He made Anne (and no doubt Margot too) read the classics of German literature, even though she found reading German difficult. He probably explained that the aim of their daily studies was to prevent them from having to catch up and repeat classes at school later, but the real reason must have been to give Margot, Anne, and Peter a set timetable for the day. Anne understood that, and once explicitly describes her studies as *time killers.*

How did Otto Frank occupy his own time? Of course, he continued to look after his firm. Kugler and Kleiman discussed any problems that came up with him, and we can assume that he made the decisions. He also read a great deal, especially *serious, rather dry descriptions of people and places,* as Anne Frank recorded on May 16, 1944, under the heading *What Our Annex Family Is Interested In.* He was always reading Dickens. Anne mentions that fact four times in her diary. For instance, she describes him sitting in a quiet corner *with his eternal Dickens,* and on another occasion *Father is sitting*

**68**    (with Dickens and the dictionary, of course) on the edge of the
sagging, squeaky bed.

Why do I emphasize this point? It brings me closer to Otto
Frank and makes me see him as a less impersonal figure. I
imagine he fled to Dickens to escape from the responsibility
he often found hard to bear. Why Dickens in particular? Was
it the humor of Dickens or the combination of realism and
fairy tale in his books that particularly appealed to Otto
Frank? Or was he fascinated by Dickens's championing of the
imprisoned and rejected members of society and children living in wretched circumstances? For whatever reason, there
must have been something in Otto Frank himself that made
Dickens his favorite reading.

Almost everything Anne says about her father in the diary
suggests an extraordinary degree of self-control and self-
sacrifice. When she writes about him, Anne mentions personal matters only occasionally, saying for instance that *his
rheumatism must have been bothering him*, or that he seems depressed. Once she says he was angry, but she cannot have
meant an outburst of rage; it must have been suppressed
anger. Sometimes, however, her comments betray the effort
necessary for so much self-control: *Father walks around with
his lips pressed together.* (October 17, 1943)

In fact, life in the Frank family always seems to have been a
disciplined affair, for when Anne first heard Mr. and Mrs. van
Pels involved in noisy argument she wrote that she could not
imagine her parents shouting at each other like that.

Anne was very obviously "Daddy's girl," and knew it, although jealousy of Margot often shows through in her diary
entries. She made great efforts to attract her father's love and
attention, and broke free of him with difficulty and relatively

late. Only her relationship with Peter, and Otto Frank's reaction to it, made her see how self-control and detachment could be a kind of rejection—or at least a rejection of intimacy. She saw that real closeness is impossible if only one partner in a relationship is open and outgoing, for if the other partner says nothing about himself or herself then at some point the one who is willing to talk will be forced into silence too. Detachment stifles these loving impulses that create intimacy. Most of the time, however, Anne (like Miep) admired Otto Frank's patience and self-discipline, qualities he must have possessed in abundance, though we should remember that both these assessments came from women and his were the virtues expected of a man at the time. In fact, I think men very often used to be seen in a rosy light by most women—wives, daughters, or others who were related to them—and that was in line with the attitude expected of both sexes.

Years later, after his return from Auschwitz and when he was back working in the firm, Anne's father made a very different impression on Miep Gies: "Since his return, Otto Frank had become once more the slightly nervous, soft-spoken man he'd been before the hiding time. The change that had taken place when he'd gone into hiding, the calm, authoritative personality he'd assumed, had vanished."[39]

Anne Frank was far more critical of her mother than of her father.

Judging by her photographs and Miep's description, Edith Frank had dark hair worn in a loose bun at the nape of her neck and parted in the center. She had dark eyes, a broad face, a wide forehead, and as she was slightly overweight she had "a sturdy, motherly look."[40] Miep Gies, who tried hard to

70    be objective and impartial in her book, several times mentions the impression Edith Frank made on her. Mrs. Frank,
she says, had come to the firm's offices with Anne soon after
arriving in Amsterdam, and "presented herself as one would
who came from a cultured, wealthy background—aloof but
sincere."[41] Later on, Miep and her fiancé, Jan Gies, were often
asked to share a meal with the Franks. Mrs. Frank would behave in a reserved, ladylike way, but she liked talking about
her childhood in Aachen, her wedding to Otto Frank, and
their time in Frankfurt, which seems to have been a happy
period for her.

Going into hiding must have been particularly hard for a
woman like Edith Frank. Used to a precisely defined role in
life, and above all to upholding the dignity of the family, she
must have felt the ground had given way beneath her feet.
She had always had a close family life (her mother lived with
the Franks until her death in January 1942), and when the
German occupation made visits between the Netherlands and
other countries impossible, at least the members of the family
could keep in touch with one another by letter. The Franks
also had an extensive circle of friends and acquaintances,
most of them German immigrants. Edith Frank invited them
to meals, to coffee, and was very much the lady of the house.
She also played an active part in the liberal Jewish community
of Amsterdam. She had been brought up to this kind of life; it
suited her own understanding of her female role, and she
drew her sense of her own value from performing such "duties."

At home, of course, she also ran the household and
brought up the children, but in the Secret Annex she had to
give up some of these activities. Mrs. van Pels (whom Anne

called Mrs. van Daan), to some extent, stole her role as housewife. It is not quite clear exactly how and why, but it must have happened quite early, for Anne Frank describes the situation on August 9, 1943, writing about her mother: *No one has the impression, as they do with Mrs. van Daan, that this is a housewife. What's the difference between the two? Well, Mrs. van D. does the cooking and Mother does the dishes and polishes the furniture.*

Mrs. van Pels was the *"queen of the kitchen,"* while Edith Frank did more menial jobs. Was Mrs. van Pels simply better at keeping house, so that Edith abandoned the field to her without a struggle? Probably, since Anne mentions only minor irritations and quarrels, not real fights. However, it is obvious that the initially friendly relationship between the two women mentioned by Miep Gies soon changed. Naturally they showed no open rivalry. Mrs. Frank would never have done that; it was "not the way to behave." It would all have been under the surface, and that would not have improved matters.

Even in child-rearing—something that must have mattered to Edith Frank, who held progressive views on the subject— she was not unchallenged. During the period of more than two years they spent in the Secret Annex, she had a number of arguments with Mr. and Mrs. van Pels, but in particular with Mrs. van Pels, who attacked Edith Frank's "modern methods" of child rearing and made fun of her.

Of course, Edith Frank's difficulties with Anne made her life in the Secret Annex no easier. Anne herself often commented on her relationship with her mother, to whom she did not feel really close. *There's one thing I can't do*, she wrote, *and that's to love Mother with the devotion of a child.* However, she did occasionally show some understanding of Edith. Once,

72    for instance, she asks herself whether any parents can be
      wholly satisfactory to their children, and on January 2, 1944,
      after rereading some earlier entries, she writes:

> It's true, she [Mother] didn't understand me, but I didn't un-
> derstand her either. Because she loved me, she was tender and
> affectionate, but because of the difficult situations I put her in,
> and the sad circumstances in which she found herself, she was
> nervous and irritable, so I can understand why she was often
> short with me. [. . .] Those violent outbursts on paper are sim-
> ply expressions of anger that, in normal life, I could have
> worked off by locking myself in my room and stamping my
> foot a few times or calling Mother names behind her back.

Four days later she explains what she dislikes about her
mother's behavior. *I've suddenly realized what's wrong with her.
Mother has said that she sees us more as friends than as daughters. That's all very nice, of course, except that a friend can't take
the place of a mother. I need my mother to set a good example
and be a person I can respect.*

Edith Frank, who was suffering severely from a sense of in-
security anyway, must have seen Anne's obvious rejection as a
failure of her efforts at child rearing. She did not live long
enough to find out whether, once the umbilical cord was finally cut, her daughter might have been able to build a new
kind of relationship with her.

In the Secret Annex Edith Frank had little left of all that
had very probably made up her previous life. Perhaps she did
not even have much left of her role as a wife. However, Anne
says little that is either positive or negative on that subject, al-

though she sometimes expresses her doubts about a close re- lationship between her parents.

To make matters even worse for Edith Frank, it is unlikely that she could draw on her own resources. Reading and studying, the two occupations that loomed so large (perhaps *too* large) for the rest of the family while they were in hiding, are unlikely to have been as important to her, although under the heading of *What Our Annex Family Is Interested In* Anne noted: *Mrs. Frank: A correspondence course in English; reads everything except detective stories.*

The picture Miep Gies draws of Edith Frank changes during the time the family spent in hiding. She continued to be quiet and friendly, but according to Miep's account (which carries conviction) she seemed to be increasingly depressed. She was sad and dispirited and nothing could cheer her up. Even the successes of the Allies, eagerly followed by the rest of them, left Edith Frank cold. She saw a dark future and could not be persuaded to shake off her cares and anxieties. There are two remarks in Miep's book that convey Edith Frank's frame of mind particularly well (it may have been genuine clinical depression): "[. . .] As much as all of us argued against her view, she saw no light at the end of the tunnel"[42]; and: "[. . .] I would leave her sitting in that room wearing a look of gloom and depression."[43]

Edith Frank badly needed to unburden herself of her fears and her despair by talking to someone. Presumably she felt she could not talk to her husband, who would probably have fended off any attempt she made to express her hopelessness in words (he would not have done so roughly, of course, but with soothing remarks). In hiding, they could not afford to

74    infect each other with discouragement and despair. As a result Edith talked to Miep, who tells us: "In a dark voice, she
would express the fear-laden thoughts that she was secretly
harboring. 'Miep, I see no end coming,' she would say. Once
she said, 'Miep, remember this: Germany will not come out of
this war the same way it went into it.' I would listen with a
sympathetic ear to whatever Mrs. Frank needed to say."[44]

   Edith Frank also complained to Miep about Mrs. van Pels,
which again was unusual. Miep writes that this was something "no one else had ever done about anyone in the Annex
for my ears. If there were tensions and conflicts, they were
never aired when one of us was visiting the hiding place."[45]
Restraint was the rule among the families in hiding; we can
assume that Otto Frank would not have allowed any indiscre-
tion.

   Miep must sometimes have found these conversations with
Edith Frank uncomfortable, for the open expression of personal suffering and despair was outside the usual carefully
observed rules of the game between the Jews in hiding and
their helpers. The pressure on Edith Frank must have been
very great for her to break down the inhibitions of her own
upbringing so far as to complain about her problems to a
woman who was not even a member of her family.

   It is strange that Anne did not notice her mother's depression, but instead regarded her as obtrusive, insensitive, and
aggressive. However, that may have been because of Anne's
age at the time. Adolescent girls often feel a need to erect
barriers against their parents—in particular their mothers. If
Anne had understood the situation and her mother's mental
state, she could hardly have erected those emotional barriers
while they were living in such confined conditions. Anger

and rage are emotions that give strength; sympathy, on the other hand, is rather debilitating and Anne could not afford it, since she was (of necessity) so determined to be strong. Certainly it was not insensitivity that led her to see her mother in such an unfair and inaccurate light. She was simply not yet strong enough to bear the suffering of others. And she had a right to look after herself; she was still a child, after all, and she needed to grow and develop.

We need to bear this in mind when we look at Anne's verdict on the other three grown-ups in hiding, because—sympathize with Anne as we may—she was certainly merciless and sometimes unjust in her comments about Mrs. van Pels and Mr. Pfeffer in particular. Perhaps her lack of sympathy was inevitable in view of her keen powers of observation and her gift for writing with precision and concentration on the essentials.

# 9 Mr. and Mrs. Van Pels

## "ALWAYS AT LOGGERHEADS"

The Franks had known the van Pels family for quite a long time before they went into hiding together, although it had probably been a rather superficial social acquaintanceship. Mr. van Pels was born in 1890 in Gehrde in Lower Saxony, the son of Dutch Jewish parents, and had fled from Osnabrück to the Netherlands with his wife and his son to escape the Nazis.

In 1938 he was hired by Otto Frank and Johannes Kleiman as an expert on spices and seasonings. Otto Frank had just founded a new, small company, Pectacon, that made seasoning mixtures for sausages; Opekta's trade in jelling agents was confined to the summer months, and Otto Frank wanted to give the company a broader base.

When he joined the company, Mr. van Pels, according to Miep's account, was a well-dressed man in his mid-forties who walked with a slight stoop and had a manly, open face and not much hair left. He was always ready to crack a joke, and was a pleasant, sociable character who fitted easily into office life. He liked telling funny stories and laughing. Miep emphasizes the fact that he was a chain-smoker. Whenever the helpers entered the Secret Annex, he always asked his usual question about cigarettes before anyone else could say a word. Anne's diaries also frequently mention his smoking and his addiction to cigarettes. He must have suffered severely in hiding, for cigarettes and tobacco were not always available.

Anne, who had looked forward very much to the arrival of the van Pels family, was complaining only five weeks after they moved in that she and Mr. van Pels were always at loggerheads. A month later she mentions in an entry that he had recently shown that he liked cats, and she approves of that. The tension between the two of them seems to have died down quickly; at least, Anne hardly complains about him anymore. When she mentions him it is usually in the course of some story or other. Mr. van Pels certainly joined in a number of arguments, but Anne did not see him as the one who started them or she would have said so at some point. In her comments on "squabbles" she usually speaks of husband and wife together as "the van Daans"—for instance, when they were dividing up the food unfairly at breakfast. This sort of thing annoys her, and she thinks "the van Daans" should be given a taste of their own medicine. However, her parents disliked fights too much to complain. Once she mentions that Mr. van Pels is "grouchy" because of the cigarette shortage, and on another occasion she says that *he has a scratchy throat, but he's making an enormous to-do over it*. Not until August 9, 1943, describing mealtimes in the Secret Annex, does she speak of him in the mocking tone she generally employs for anyone who has annoyed her. *His opinion is the best, he knows the most about everything. Granted, the man has a good head on his shoulders, but it's swelled to no small degree.*

In the same entry, however, she says that he reacts violently

78    to contradiction and *can hiss like a cat . . . but I'd rather he
didn't. Once you've seen it, you never want to see it again.* Perhaps this is why she did not let herself get annoyed with him
as often as with Mrs. van Pels and Mr. Pfeffer. Perhaps she felt
she was not up to his weight—I don't mean intellectually, but
in terms of aggression. After all, it was not usual for people in
her own family to voice their own wishes and insist on them
as vehemently as Mr. van Pels. For instance, he didn't give up
smoking even when it was necessary to economize and valuable items had to be sold.

Anne Frank had not learned to parry such vigorous self-
assertion; it must have seemed strange to her and would have
made her cautious in her dealings with Mr. van Pels. At any
rate, she writes on March 25, 1944, that you could *win Mr.
van Daan over to your side by agreeing with him, listening qui-
etly, not saying much and most of all . . . responding to his teas-
ing and his corny jokes with a joke of your own.* This seems to
have been the strategy she adopted soon after their first few
clashes.

Mr. and Mrs. van Pels were involved in many of the dis-
putes in the Secret Annex, and they often had loud arguments
with each other. Their quarrels, however, always ended in *the
"oh, my sweet Putti" and "darling Kerli" stage of reconciliation.*
There must have been a number of disagreements between
Mr. van Pels and Mrs. Frank, although Anne gives no details
(out of discretion or simply because she wasn't interested?).
For instance, she remarks on January 15, 1944: *Mother has
expressed a wish, which isn't likely to come true any time soon:
not to have to see Mr. van Daan's face for two whole weeks.*

The restless, active Mr. van Pels must have suffered from
his confinement. In addition, like Edith Frank and his wife,

he may not have been able to bury himself very easily in intellectual pursuits. At least, under the heading of *What Our Annex Family Is Interested In*, Anne notes: *Mr. van Daan: No courses; looks up many things in Knaur's Encyclopedia and Lexicon; likes to read detective stories, medical books and love stories, exciting or trivial.* He seems to have been an impulsive man, perhaps not very well educated, who could not rely on his own resources to any great extent. His abilities were certainly useful in his job, but he must have found it hard to bear an inactive life. I imagine him like a wolf shut in a cage, pacing silently back and forth.

Miep Gies has remarkably little to say about Mrs. van Pels. "Mrs. van Pels was temperamental, flirty, chatty."[46] After reading Anne's diary one has to agree with this verdict, but it describes only a part of Mrs. van Pels's character. She was more than simply temperamental, flirtatious, and talkative; she was also industrious, cheerful, impulsive, and eager to please.

Soon after the van Pels family moved in, Anne writes of *friction* caused by the pettiness of Mrs. van Pels. For instance, says Anne, she took her own sheets out of their communal linen cupboard to save them for later on, after the war. (Mrs. Frank then removed her own sheets, too.) Furthermore, Mrs. van Pels was "miffed" because her china was being used instead of the Franks'. (Although one wonders just how that happened, since the Franks moved into the Secret Annex first, and their china must have been in use then. Presumably they packed it away before Mr. and Mrs. van Pels arrived. Who was being petty now?)

Disagreements between the two women therefore began very early. Were they trying to establish a pecking order? Mrs. Frank would hardly have needed to compete—or did she? Or

80    was there something quite different involved—for instance, physical attraction? Miep describes Frau van Pels as a pretty and rather flirtatious woman, while Edith Frank had a "sturdy, motherly look" because she "carried a few extra pounds."[47] We know from Anne, who kept a jealous eye open for it, that Mrs. van Pels sometimes tried to flirt with Otto Frank. Were Mrs. Frank and Mrs. van Pels rivals in some way, inappropriate as that may seem in view of the situation?

All we learn from the diaries (where we read about it at length) is that Mrs. van Pels had a limited mind, was hot-tempered, vain, and talkative, and frequently argued about the way to bring up children.

Mrs. van Pels had given Peter a traditional upbringing, including corporal punishment. On May 11, 1944, Anne quotes her: *"He wasn't like this at home," she said. "I'd have belted him so hard he'd have gone flying down the stairs (!). He's never been so insolent. This isn't the first time he's deserved a good hiding."* Anne's parents did not hit her—at least, not now that she was in her teens—and even earlier any corporal punishment would have amounted to a slap at the most. There were differences, then, between the two families' views on child rearing.

Anne describes frequent quarrels and makes no secret of her contempt for Mrs. van Pels, but she gradually noticed (and admitted in her diary) that Mrs. van Pels also had her good points. She was hardworking and cheerful, at least most of the time. Even her arrival at the Secret Annex caused amusement because she had brought her chamber pot, explaining that she didn't feel at home without it. And she liked to tell funny stories of her young days, *entertaining us with some bit of nonsense or other*, which made them laugh.

Edith Frank with her daughters, Anne (left) and Margot, on
the Hauptwache, a famous square in the center of Frankfurt
am Main, 1933

Otto Frank, Anne's father,
May 1936

Edith Frank-Holländer, Anne's
mother, May 1935

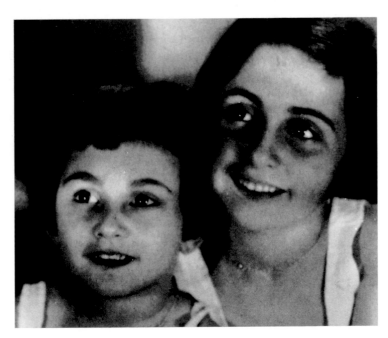

Anne Frank (left) and her sister, Margot, 1933

Margot (left) and Anne Frank, 1940

Anne Frank on the roof of her house in Merwedeplein, 1940

An entry in the Diary: *This is a photograph of me as I wish I looked all the time. Then I might still have a chance of getting to Hollywood. But at present, I'm afraid, I usually look quite different.*
Anne Frank, October 10, 1942

Peter van Pels

Fritz Pfeffer

Johannes Kleiman and Victor Kugler

Miep Gies (left) and Bep Voskuijl

Anne Frank, 1941

The room Anne Frank shared with Fritz Pfeffer

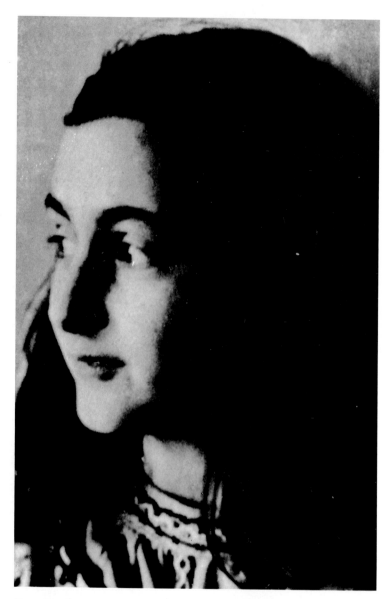

Anne Frank, 1941

There was not much laughter otherwise in the Secret Annex. (Were Mr. van Pels's funny stories really sidesplitting?) Of course the situation of the Jews in hiding was very serious, but laughter was probably not especially common in the Frank family anyway. Anne fretted, longing to have a really good laugh again, the way she used to laugh with her girl-friends. On September 16, 1943, she writes: *A good hearty laugh would help more than ten valerian drops,\* but we've almost forgotten how to laugh.*

Mrs. van Pels too was largely excluded from the absorbing occupations of reading and studying, but she did study Dutch and English, not very successfully, and according to Anne she read a biography or a novel now and then.

Anne did not think much of Mrs. van Pels's intellectual abilities (showing a superior attitude not at all uncommon in intelligent girls of her age), and she also thought her immodest, egotistic, calculating, vain, and flirtatious. However, Miep saw her in a different light; she thought her grateful and generous. On Miep's birthday in February 1944, Mrs. van Pels gave her a beautiful antique ring to show her gratitude, and she did it privately, without any showing off in front of the others. This was at a time when Kleiman was already having to sell valuable items for Mr. and Mrs. van Pels because their savings had run out.

Mrs. van Pels was certainly not a particularly clever or well-educated woman, but her cheerfulness and unflagging attention to the housekeeping were probably more important than Anne Frank realized in the daily life of the Secret Annex. Anne herself knew that her verdict on Mrs. van Pels was at

---

*Valerian drops: a sedative used to calm nervousness.

82    least in part unfair. On January 22, 1944, she wrote: *Mrs. van Daan is by no means a wonderful person, yet half the arguments could have been avoided if Mother hadn't been so hard to deal with every time they got onto a tricky subject. Mrs. van Daan does have one good point, though: you can talk to her.* And she adds on March 25, 1944: *Father and Mother's biggest mistake in dealing with the van Daans is that they're never candid and friendly (admittedly, the friendliness might have to be feigned).* She thought that Mrs. van Pels could be *won over by talking openly to her and admitting when you're wrong.* She would also admit frankly to her faults, of which she had many—surely quite a considerable virtue.

Unlike Mrs. Frank, Mrs. van Pels could obviously derive a sense of her own worth from her role as housewife. She probably felt that even if the household tasks often got on her nerves, they did at least keep her occupied. Anne quotes her on March 14, 1944: *"I'd stopped wanting to be queen of the kitchen long ago. But sitting around doing nothing was boring, so I went back to cooking. Still, I can't help complaining: it's impossible to cook without oil, and all those disgusting smells make me sick to my stomach. Besides, what do I get in return for my efforts? Ingratitude and rude remarks. I'm always the black sheep; I get blamed for everything."*

Two women, Edith Frank and Frau van Pels, neither of whom had presumably ever learned to show solidarity with her own sex: there was bound to be rivalry and jealousy between them. From the viewpoint of a woman today, one can only feel sorry for them and think it was a pity, for they could have helped each other so much.

# 10 Mr. Pfeffer

## "ALL HE CAN THINK ABOUT IS HIS CHARLOTTE"

Anne Frank's comments on Fritz Pfeffer (called Albert Dussel in her diary), with whom she shared her room, are even harsher and more merciless. He was born in 1889 and had left Germany in 1938. He lived with Charlotte Kaletta, a non-Jewish woman. Since his position would have been more secure as a "married man of mixed race," the couple now desperately tried to marry, but they did not succeed. Ever since the passing of the infamous anti-Jewish Nuremberg Laws, marriage and indeed any other relationship between "Aryans" and Jews had been prohibited.

Mr. Pfeffer belonged to the Franks' wider circle of acquaintances. Miep had met him in their apartment and had become his patient. She liked him both personally and as a dentist, and describes him as a handsome, charming man bearing some resemblance to the French singer Maurice Chevalier.[48]

Anne Frank's account of the way in which he came to join the people in the Secret Annex was that when the news of raids and deportations grew worse and worse, the two families in hiding told each other that where there was food enough for seven people there would be enough for eight,

**84** and they decided to offer one more person shelter. Their only qualms were that it would place an even greater burden on Kugler and Kleiman, but Otto Frank spoke to them and they agreed. *"It's just as dangerous, whether there are seven or eight,"* they noted rightly.

Again according to Anne, the people in the Secret Annex discussed the matter and chose the dentist Dr. Fritz Pfeffer. They knew him slightly and liked him. He was to sleep in the girls' room with Anne, while Margot took the folding bed from the attic and moved into the room next door with her parents. Anne did not much like the idea of sharing her room with Mr. Pfeffer, but she agreed with the others that sacrifices had to be made in times like these.

Miep's account of the story is rather different. According to her, Mr. Pfeffer approached her first to ask if she knew anywhere he could hide. She promised to try to find somewhere and asked Otto Frank the next day. "Mr. Frank listened to my news with interest—because Pfeffer and his wife* had been among the refugees from Germany who used to come to the Franks' Saturday-afternoon gatherings. I knew Mr. Frank was as fond of him as I was.

"I thought nothing else about this exchange of information until several days later, during my afternoon visit to the hiding place. Mr. Frank said he had something to discuss with me. I sat down and Mr. Frank said, 'Miep, where seven can eat, eight people can eat as well. All of us have talked this over and we've decided that Pfeffer can come and join us here in our hiding place. But he must come first thing tomorrow morning.' "[49]

---

* Miep Gies refers to Charlotte Kaletta as Fritz Pfeffer's "wife." However, they were not, in fact, married.

He did not in fact arrive next day, but a few days later on November 16, 1942, and from then until the Jews hiding in the Secret Annex were arrested, Miep kept Pfeffer and Charlotte Kaletta in touch with each other, although she did not tell Charlotte where he was. She writes: "Beginning right away, I met once a week with Dr. Pfeffer's wife, a charming blond woman one year older than I, and delivered his thick letters to her. She would give me letters, books, parcels, and bits of dental equipment that he had requested. She was a Christian, and because she no longer had a Jew with her, she was in no danger. [. . .] I pretended to know nothing about where Fritz Pfeffer was hiding. However, Mrs. Pfeffer was a discreet and sensitive person; she knew better than to search out information."[50]

On the one hand we have a man like Fritz Pfeffer in his fifties, probably already relatively inflexible and set in his ways, plucked for a second time from his familiar surroundings and the dental practice he had been illicitly conducting, unused to the company of children; and on the other we have an impulsive, sharp-tongued girl like Anne Frank. They were sharing a small room for better or worse; it could hardly be anything but for worse.

Pfeffer was very soon getting on Anne Frank's nerves. He was always giving her cause for complaint; she could not see a single point in his favor. Even the pseudonym of "Dussel" that she gave him can only be seen as contemptuous, since in German it means a fool or idiot. Anne obviously could not resist this intentional slur, although she did not usually indulge in puns.

If only because of his status as a dentist, a well-regarded profession, Pfeffer was used to being seen as a man of some authority, but everything was different now. At home, says Anne, his word was law, which did not suit her at all. She did not like the fact that he was a "tattletale" and singled out her mother as the *recipient of his reports*. She accused him of stupidity, failure to conform to the rules of their hiding place, greed, and secretiveness. He had hidden the bread, cheese, jam, and eggs his Charlotte sent him in his cupboard, she writes on May 1, 1943, adding reproachfully: *It's absolutely disgraceful that Dussel, whom we've treated with such kindness and whom we took in to save from destruction, should stuff himself behind our backs and not give us anything. After all, we've shared all we had with him!* And on August 3, 1943, she notes, with all the arrogance of a fourteen-year-old: *Dussel is slipping lower and lower in my estimation, and he's already below zero. Whatever he says about politics, history, geography or anything else is so ridiculous that I hardly dare repeat it.*

He could do no right as far as she was concerned. Whatever he said or did was wrong. I must admit to feeling sorry for him. He may have been a difficult and obstinate character, but he had little chance of doing himself justice and winning approval in the Secret Annex. The main reason, of course, was that he was on his own. The others formed family groups and if necessary could always rely on family solidarity. Anne was well aware of that fact and made use of it in her quarrels with the van Pels family. Fritz Pfeffer had no one, and not even a room where he could be by himself. He was always in the company of the pert and badly behaved Anne, who watched him suspiciously, always ready to pounce on whatever stupid thing he said or did next, or so he must have felt. The two groups of the Frank and van Pels families confronted him separately or together, depending on the situation, rejecting him and blaming him. And then there were the three young people, not an indissoluble group but sometimes banding together in their dislike of him. In fact, it is perfectly possible that Anne, Margot, and Peter transferred onto Pfeffer those feelings of aggression toward their parents that they could not afford to indulge in the Secret Annex.

No wonder he spent so much time in the bathroom. No wonder he refused to stop corresponding with Charlotte Kaletta and a few other people, although he was reproached for it by his companions in hiding, who thought it endangered them all.

How did Mr. Pfeffer spend his time? Anne writes: *Mr. Dussel: Is learning English, Spanish and Dutch with no noticeable results; reads everything; goes along with the opinion of the majority.* She accuses him of conformity, but what else could he have done if he wanted to avoid the frequent quarrels going on around him?

For two years, Fritz Pfeffer was the loneliest of all the people in the Secret Annex. Even if we accept that he gave the others plenty of reasons to attack him and there was good cause for friction, we have to feel sorry for him. There is no doubt that he became a scapegoat.

The group as a whole should not be seen as some kind of commune; they had become a community only as an emergency measure. They did not go into hiding of their own free will, nor had all their members been at liberty to make up their own minds. The group was formed by chance rather than choice; they had worked together, they knew each other, they liked each other. That was about all there was to it.

In the circumstances splinter groups were bound to form, and they tended to split into traditional family factions. Even

**88**   Anne, Margot, and Peter only occasionally managed to break that mold, so what chance did Pfeffer have? And with whom could he have joined up? Otto Frank was so detached; his wife was moody and perhaps, as Anne once said, even cynical. The stiff and starchy Pfeffer cannot have got on particularly well with the rather outspoken, impulsive Mr. van Pels, so that really left only Mrs. van Pels. A little flattery would always win her over, but she was unreliable. Under the date of November 3, 1943, Anne Frank describes a quarrel between Pfeffer and Mrs. van Pels: *When Dussel is talking about Mrs. van D., he invariably calls her "that old bat" or "that stupid hag," and conversely, Mrs. van D. refers to our ever so learned gentleman as an "old maid" or a "touchy neurotic spinster," etc.*

On another occasion, however, June 5, 1944, we read: *Close friendship between the latter [Dussel] and Mrs. van Daan, flirtations, kisses and friendly little smiles. Dussel is beginning to long for female companionship.* Anne's explanation could have been right—two years of celibacy may have been an additional problem for Pfeffer, and one that did not affect the other adults in hiding. However, his advances to Mrs. van Pels could also have been a clumsy attempt to find an ally. But as usual when he put himself forward in any way, he was laughed at and mocked.

Fritz Pfeffer's character and isolation marked him for the role of victim, and his upbringing probably prevented him from expressing his loneliness and suffering; perhaps he could not even admit it to himself. His is a sad story.

# 11 Margot

## "A PARAGON OF VIRTUE"

There is not much to say about Margot. I do not mean she was an insignificant character, but like Peter she remains strangely colorless in both Anne's diary and Miep's book. The reason was her reserve and *diffidence*—a word Anne uses to describe anyone who does not demand attention, who keeps in the background and does not want anything for herself. This attitude certainly seems to have been characteristic of Margot.

Miep says only that Margot, like Anne, helped with the cooking and cleaning and was always reading and studying. All through the long period of hiding, Miep mentions no personal relationship between herself and Margot, whom she describes as "quite withdrawn." Margot did not ask for things, express personal wishes, or seem to need intimate conversation. (One suspects that she was very like her father.) In addition she was quite often unwell, even before the family went into hiding, but nothing could keep her away from her schoolwork. This quotation from Miep is typical; "Margot too was very low, so silent and undemonstrative. Always kind, and always helpful, Margot had a way of making herself invis-

90 ible. She never got in the way; she made no demands."[51] The most intimate detail about Margot recorded by Miep is that she put curlers in her hair. (So did Anne, who also bleached the hairs on her upper lip.)

For a long time Anne herself does not seem to have felt particularly friendly toward her sister, much as she may once have admired her, as Miep tells us. Those days were over, and Anne was no longer the little sister hanging on Margot's every word. She thought Margot was too well behaved or, we might say today, too well adjusted. Margot was the clever one who always had good grades and hardly ever did anything to annoy her parents. She was a *paragon of virtue* in every respect; it got on Anne's nerves and drew mockery from her.

Anne also obviously suffered from the normal childish jealousy of a younger sister for an older one who was allowed, for instance, to read books still forbidden to herself. In Anne's opinion, Margot was always the favorite child of their parents—particularly their mother. On October 14, 1942, she says for the first time—and in this form of wording the only time—that her mother, she, and Margot were the best of friends again; but only three weeks later, on November 7, she is writing of Margot's cross temper and her own annoyance at her parents' preference for her sister. *Margot just happens to be the smartest, the kindest, the prettiest and the best. But I have a right to be taken seriously too.* She adds that she isn't jealous, but that seems doubtful, even if we can well believe that Anne did not want to be weak-willed and passive, as she describes her sister. Margot, she says, would always let herself be persuaded by others and was always giving way. She didn't want to be like that; she wanted to *have more backbone*.

For some time Margot appears in Anne's diary only in connection with normal family concerns, but on January 12, 1944, Anne notes: *Margot's gotten much nicer. She seems a lot different than she used to be. She's not nearly as catty these days and is becoming a real friend. She no longer thinks of me as a little kid who doesn't count.*

From now on the relationship between the sisters changed, although Anne avoided too much intimacy with Margot. She pointed out (and I think rightly) that they were always together anyway and she didn't want her close friend with her all the time. Anne's reluctance to tell Margot anything too intimate and personal must also have concealed a fear, not unjustified in their cramped living conditions, that Margot might later use something she had said against her unintentionally, or out of thoughtlessness, or in a quarrel. An important factor in the improvement of their relationship was that Margot too was now beginning to detach herself from her mother—considerably later than Anne. According to eyewitness accounts, Anne and Margot were very close to each other at the last, in Auschwitz and Bergen-Belsen.

So how did Margot spend her time? How did she manage to remain so "invisible"? Under the heading *What Our Annex Family Is Interested In* we find the following list for Margot: *Margot Frank: Correspondence courses in English, French and Latin, shorthand in English, German and Dutch, trigonometry, solid geometry, mechanics, physics, chemistry, algebra, geometry, English literature, French literature, German literature, Dutch literature, bookkeeping, geography, modern history, biology, economics; reads everything, preferably on religion and medicine.*

Margot studied hard, as Miep confirms, and according to Miep she had enjoyed schoolwork even before she went into hiding. She was falling back on what seemed her established

**92**   role—a role that had presumably always earned her admiration and approval (though Anne once mentions that her
mother and father were not like other parents about grades
and didn't mind if a report card was good or bad). One suspects from Margot's long list of interests that she was escaping
into her studies. Perhaps they had become an obsession with
her—a way of avoiding possible unpleasant scenes and emotions and blotting them out, just as her father sought refuge
in Dickens and Anne escaped into her diary.

Had Margot no dreams and wishes of her own? All Anne
says is that what Margot most wanted when they were free
again was to lie for over half an hour in a hot bath filled to the
brim, and that her ambition was to nurse babies in Palestine.
To Anne, this was a modest ambition. She herself wanted to
spend a year in Paris and a year in London learning languages
and studying art history; she wanted to see more of the world.

I find Margot's diffidence and withdrawal depressing. What
did she do with her emotions, her own wishes, the annoyance
she must sometimes have felt with her obviously much more
lively sister? In one of her last entries, on July 6, 1944, Anne
writes: *Margot and Peter are always saying to me, "If I had your
spunk and your strength, if I had your drive and unflagging energy, I could . . . !"*

Margot was well aware that she was unable to live out the
"other" side of her nature, but she lacked either the will or
the energy to do anything about it. Perhaps she would have
been different if she had been surrounded by friends and in-
vigorated by a normal social life at school and at home. We
will never know. But it is clear that her patience and discipline would have made her well suited to become a nurse for
babies in Palestine.

# 12 Peter

## "I CREATED AN IMAGE IN MY MIND"

We do not learn much from Anne's diary about Peter either—I mean the real Peter van Pels and his preferences, thoughts, and feelings. Anne invented "her" Peter, the boy she needed because she wanted a love story. It could almost be called a poetic act of creation. His glance, his smile, and his silence were enough for her to create someone with the intellectual qualities she longed for. But that was not until later, in 1944.

According to Miep Gies the real Peter, not the Peter of Anne's invention, was a good-looking, strongly built boy with thick dark hair, dreamy eyes (whatever she meant by that), and a sweet nature. He was as quiet and withdrawn as Margot, very introspective, and he always kept in the background. He liked making things and often used to go to the attic, where he had set up a workshop for himself. Miep is two-thirds of the way through her book before she says anything at all personal about him: just before Anne's fifteenth birthday he gave Miep a few coins and asked her to buy Anne some pretty flowers. Then she noticed how big and strong he looked and how nicely his brown hair curled. "Sweet boy, I thought." (This account may, of course, be colored by Anne's

**94**   picture of Peter as presented in her diary.) In any case, Peter's most striking qualities seem to have been reserve and silence—and he thereby offered Anne the perfect opportunity to invent a character for him. Anyone who says little may be thinking the most elevated of thoughts; at least he provides no evidence to the contrary.

Directly after his arrival Anne described him as a rather boring, shy boy, not quite sixteen, of whom not much could be expected. Even a week later she was not thinking any better of him. She did not take him seriously; she made fun of his alleged hypochondria, credited him with an unfortunate liking for foreign words, and complained that he and Margot were so boring and quiet they weren't really young at all. Both of them were always being held up to her as an example, which she thought *horrible*. In the cramped conditions of the Secret Annex, reserved and inconspicuous behavior must have been a virtue valued even more highly than in normal circumstances. There were problems enough without having loud, pushy children around the place.

Peter made no trouble and gave no one any problems, if we leave aside a few relatively harmless conflicts with his parents—for instance when he was not allowed to read a certain book but read it surreptitiously all the same. Otherwise he avoided arguments, and of all the people in the Secret Annex, he took least part in the constant bickering.

We cannot tell from the diary whether Peter was a problem to himself. On the occasion of the first loud argument between Mr. and Mrs. van Pels on September 2, 1942, Anne comments only: *Of course, it's very difficult for Peter, who gets caught in the middle.* However, this almost sympathetic remark is immediately canceled out: *But no one takes Peter seri-*

*ously anymore, since he's hypersensitive and lazy.* Whether this "laziness" refers to work or study is not quite clear. In any case, Peter seems to have seen to all kinds of practical details in a quiet way. Anne mentions—in passing, and without making much of it—that he had nailed a cushion to the top of a door frame because they all kept hitting their heads on it. He carried sacks of beans upstairs, he fetched potatoes, he checked the storeroom, he chopped wood. And he obviously took good care of his cat, Mouschi.

Until 1944, Peter does not feature very often in Anne's diary; indeed, she mentions him only when he has played the leading part in some incident that she found funny. Her comments on him are mainly derogatory; she laughs at him. But once at least she found something they had in common: they both liked dressing up and making other people laugh. She fended off any earlier attempts on his part to develop a closer relationship, or perhaps she did not understand them. She told her parents he kept stroking her cheek, and she didn't like it.

What did Peter think of all the reading and studying in the Annex? He was included in Otto Frank's study timetable, although he clearly did not plunge into intellectual pursuits with the same pleasure as Anne and Margot. On September 21, 1942, Anne notes: *Peter has taken up his English with great reluctance.* With two such academically clever girls as Anne and Margot in front of him, it must have been difficult for him to motivate himself to study. He would inevitably have felt stupid and awkward compared with the two sisters. Under the heading of *What Our Annex Family Is Interested In,* Anne writes of Peter van Pels: *Is learning English, French (correspondence course), shorthand in Dutch, English and German,*

*commercial correspondence in English, woodworking, economics
and sometimes math; seldom reads, sometimes geography.*

For a long time, about a year and a half, Anne could see
nothing in a boy who was so awkward in many ways. But
then, literally overnight, she suddenly began taking an interest in him. That interest was aroused by a dream.

Anne does speak of dreams quite often, but she usually
means longings, daydreams, dreamy moods. She very seldom
mentions real dreams: only three times in all, and all three
dreams are from the year 1944.

On January 6 she dreamed of Peter Schiff. She had been
friends with him for three months when they were in the
sixth class at primary school. She had an *out-and-out crush* on
him at the time, and even when he ceased to take an interest
in her she was still "in love" with him in secret. In her fan-
tasies she planned to marry him one day (as she wrote in her
diary before going into hiding).

On January 19 she mentions a second dream, again about
Peter Schiff.

On March 8 she dreamed of two Peters, one a little boy, the
other Peter van Pels. This dream suggests that she could not
separate her warm feelings for Peter Schiff (probably intensi-
fied in memory) from what she now felt for Peter van Pels.

The most important dream was the one on January 6. She had
dreamed that Peter Schiff pressed his cheek against hers, and
she experienced a deep sense of happiness that was still with
her when she woke up. All this time she had never thought of
Peter Schiff again, and now she felt full of love for him.

This was the dream she could not forget; it became the fo-
cus of her thoughts and feelings. Whether it was born of an
awakening need for affection and closeness or whether it

aroused that need does not matter; the point is that the dream made her aware of her own longings. She herself set great store by it, as two comments show. On January 22, 1944, not quite two weeks later, she writes: *It seems as if I've grown up since the night I had that dream, as if I've become more independent.* And two months later, on March 7, 1944, she writes: *After New Year's the second big change occurred: my dream . . .* (The first big change came when the family suddenly went into hiding. She could not have emphasized the importance of her dream more strongly.)

The consequences are obvious from her diary entry the day after she had the dream: *My longing for someone to talk to has become so unbearable that I somehow took it into my head to select Peter for this role. On the few occasions when I have gone to Peter's room during the day, I've always thought it was nice and cozy. But Peter's too polite to show someone the door when they're bothering him, so I've never dared to stay long. I've always been afraid he'd think I was a pest.*

There is no such kindly reference to Peter in any of the previous entries, and still less does Anne express any fears of bothering him. Previously she has always thought herself interesting and Peter boring. It seems he now springs to mind when she wants someone to talk to.

She writes of the second dream, also about Peter Schiff, only that it was *less vivid and not quite as beautiful as the last.* In the third, another Peter makes his appearance. On March 8 Anne writes:

*What I didn't write to Margot, but what I'll confess to you, dear Kitty, is that I've been dreaming of Peter a great deal. The night before last I dreamed I was skating right here in our liv-*

*ing room with that little boy from the Apollo ice-skating rink;
he was with his sister, the girl with the spindly legs who always wore the same blue dress. I introduced myself, overdoing
it a bit, and asked him his name. It was Peter. In my dream I
wondered just how many Peters I actually knew!*

*Then I dreamed we were standing in Peter's room, facing
each other beside the stairs. I said something to him; he gave
me a kiss, but replied that he didn't love me all that much and
that I shouldn't flirt. In a desperate and pleading voice I said,
"I'm not flirting, Peter!"*

*When I woke up I was glad Peter hadn't said it after all.*

*Last night I dreamed we were kissing each other, but Peter's
cheeks were very disappointing: they weren't as soft as they
looked. They were more like Father's cheeks—the cheeks of a
man who already shaves.*

Anne Frank was dreaming, then, of tenderness and physical
closeness. In the Secret Annex, however, there was only one
boy—Peter, the real Peter—with whom she could do anything to satisfy the emotional and sexual needs that had been
awakened so suddenly and strongly.

Of course she could not admit it to herself as plainly as
that; her upbringing and her middle-class sense of decorum
would have forbidden it. She therefore had to fall in love with
Peter in order to overcome her inhibitions, and she had to
idealize him in order to fall in love with him (not an unusual
behavior pattern even today). On January 6 she confesses to
Kitty: *But people will do almost anything to satisfy their longings; take me, for example, I've made up my mind to visit Peter
more often and, somehow, get him to talk to me.*

She did it, too. Not only did she attract Peter to her, she

also succeeded in turning a rather ordinary relationship between a sexually inexperienced boy and girl, "experimenting" with each other for lack of any other opportunities, into a genuine love story with its heights and depths, its tumultuous emotions and its moments of overwhelming happiness.

I imagine everyone of any age, whether fifteen, twenty-five, or sixty-five, will wonder in reading this love story—not a genuine love story and yet very real in Anne's mind—what exactly the two of them did together. Not only are questions about the sexual aspect of the relationship obvious, it is also legitimate for us to consider them, since these were clearly extremely important experiences for Anne and an essential part of her story.

If we follow the course of events in the diary it is clear that Anne and Peter by no means just sat dreamily side by side in the attic, hand in hand or arm in arm. They very soon went further, if only verbally at first. They discussed the male and female genital areas, apparently in general but really speaking of their own. It was the familiar children's game of "I'll show you mine if you show me yours," but on a verbal level: a highly erotic game between two young people who were no longer children. In fact, verbal eroticism fascinated Anne on a literary level too, as is shown in her entry of March 24, 1944, where she experiments with a description of the external female genitals. At a time when there was very little women's writing on such subjects, this was a very original achievement.

However, they went further. There is much to suggest that Anne and Peter progressed to a form of petting. Not the direct, full variety; in spite of arousal on both sides, they would have been too bashful for that. It was probably enough for him that they pressed close to each other, and for her that he may have touched her briefly. Reading Anne's phrasing of her entry for April 28, 1944, I assume that she experienced an orgasm, and not just heightened emotions, during one evening with Peter.

Anne was in a state of great physical and mental excitement that evening. They had been sitting on the divan in each other's arms when *suddenly the everyday Anne slipped away and the second Anne took her place. The second Anne, who's never overconfident or amusing, but wants only to love and be gentle. I sat pressed against him and felt a wave of emotion come over me. Tears rushed to my eyes [. . . ] At eight-thirty I stood up and went to the window. [. . .] I was still trembling, I was still Anne number two. [. . . ] In a daze, we embraced, over and over again, never to stop, oh!*

The same entry also contains the following passage that hints at what kind of experience it was that left Anne so shattered:

> *Is it right for me to yield so soon, for me to be so passionate, to be filled with as much passion and desire as Peter? Can I, a girl, allow myself to go that far? [. . . ] Every night, after our last kiss, I feel like running away and never looking him in the eyes again. Away, far away into the darkness and alone! [. . .] My heart is still too tender to be able to recover so quickly from a shock like the one I had last night. [. . .] Peter's reached a part of me that no one has ever reached before, except in my dream! He's taken hold of me and turned me inside out.*

The experience was enough to shatter Anne's image of herself and plunge her into a profound moral dilemma, as the final part of the entry shows.

*Am I really only fourteen? Am I really just a silly schoolgirl?*
*Am I really so inexperienced in everything? I have more expe-*
*rience than most; I've experienced something almost no one my*
*age ever has.*
*I'm afraid of myself, afraid my longing is making me yield*
*too soon. How can it ever go right with other boys later on?*
*Oh, it's so hard, the eternal struggle between heart and mind.*
*There's a time and a place for both, but how can I be sure that*
*I've chosen the right time?*

These quotations would seem to confirm my assumption:
Anne Frank experienced the first orgasm of her life and was
genuinely shaken to the core. But her entire upbringing, her
ideas of what was right (not simply of what was seemly; she
was too brave and strong for that), prevented her from describing the experience in plain terms. Her gift for language
would have enabled her to do so, as her description of the
genitals proves.

On the one hand she seems to have enjoyed the experience
very much indeed; on the other she was extremely uneasy
about it, for two reasons in particular. The change she had felt
in herself went too far for her. Her emotions and longings had
overwhelmed her; she feared for the independence and self-
control to which she clung at this difficult time. Also, she
realized that her feelings for Peter were not really strong
enough to justify such an intense sexual relationship. She remembered that it was she who had had to win Peter over.

The relationship was initiated by Anne, determined by
Anne, experienced by Anne. But at the peak of her emotion
she felt doubt rising in her and other claims making themselves heard. In her entry of April 28, 1944, she wonders

ANNE FRANK: A Hidden Life

whether she would marry Peter if she were older, and she answers the question honestly, in the negative. He has too little character, she says, too little willpower, too little courage and strength; he is still a child, emotionally no older than herself. *All he wants is happiness and peace of mind.* Although she was younger in age, she was surely more mature than Peter, and in any case much stronger.

Where did she get that extraordinary certainty, that awareness of her own value? She knew who she was, what she wanted to be, and what she could be. Her truly heroic struggle to reconcile her emotional and sexual needs and her intellectual requirements with reality is one of the finest things I have ever read about in such a young girl.

In spite of all the tension and excitement of her new experiences, Anne found the strength and maturity she needed to detach herself from Peter. She could very well have played a game that would have brought pleasure and variety into her monotonous life, but she withstood the temptation and remained true to her self-appointed aim of achieving strength of character. On May 19 she writes to Kitty: *After my laborious conquest, I've distanced myself a little from the situation, but you mustn't think my love has cooled. Peter's a sweetheart, but I've slammed the door to my inner self.*

And on Tuesday, June 13, she writes the following account:

*Sometimes I think my terrible longing for him was overexaggerated. But that's not true, because if I'm unable to go to his room for a day or two, I long for him as desperately as I ever did. Peter is kind and good, and yet I can't deny that he's disappointed me in many ways. I especially don't care for his dislike of religion, his talk of food and various things of that nature. Still, I'm firmly convinced that we'll stick to our agreement never to quarrel. Peter is peace-loving, tolerant and extremely easygoing.*

They did not quarrel, of course; Peter was undoubtedly too "peace-loving, tolerant and easygoing" for that. Anne wanted some sort of conflict even in a relationship like this. She wanted a partner who would help her to grow and become stronger. Peter was in no position to be such a partner; the attempt would have been hopelessly beyond him. It says much for Anne that she did not express her disappointment with him, blame him, or make fun of him; on the contrary, she showed concern and wondered how she could help him to become stronger himself.

I do not think she hurt Peter, though I imagine he felt some disappointment when her enthusiasm waned so quickly. But she did not abandon him entirely, and he must have felt less lonely than before. The clarity with which Anne herself saw her relationship with Peter is evident in her entry of July 15, the last to mention him.

*No, I think about Peter much more than I do Father. I know very well that he was my conquest, and not the other way round. I created an image of him in my mind, pictured him as a quiet, sweet, sensitive boy badly in need of friendship and love! I needed to pour out my heart to a living person. I wanted a friend who would help me find my way again. I accomplished what I set out to do and drew him, slowly but surely, toward me. When I finally got him to be my friend, it automatically developed into an intimacy that, when I think about it now, seems outrageous. We talked about the most pri-*

*vate things, but we haven't yet touched upon the things closest to my heart. I still can't make head or tail of Peter. Is he superficial, or is it shyness that holds him back, even with me? But putting all that aside, I made one mistake: I used intimacy to get closer to him, and in doing so, I ruled out other forms of friendship. He longs to be loved, and I can see he's beginning to like me more with each passing day. Our time together leaves him feeling satisfied, but just makes me want to start all over again. I never broach the subjects I long to bring out into the open. I forced Peter, more than he realizes, to get close to me, and now he's holding on for dear life. I honestly don't see any effective way of shaking him off and getting him back on his own two feet.*

She was barely fifteen years old when she wrote that: an age at which, had she been born in another time, she might have been attending dancing classes, going to the pictures with an "admirer," talking and giggling with her girlfriends about love and boys.

We can only speculate on what Peter thought of the whole affair. In a way he was Anne's "victim," even if it did him good. Almost all the remarks of his that Anne reports were elicited by her; she almost put them into his mouth. I think we may assume that he was not really in love with her, or he would have gone on courting her more actively. She aroused him; that is, she aroused his sexual curiosity, and Peter too must have felt an urgent sexual curiosity. He probably liked her, admired her, and felt a little afraid of her. Her romanticism would also have struck a sympathetic note in him. He was not an aggressively macho type of boy, and he too probably enjoyed sitting hand in hand, looking at the moon.

Apart from that, however, the real Peter remains a colorless
character, and even the invented picture, the romantic figure
created in Anne's mind, is not particularly lively. Inevitably,
Anne was concentrating too much on herself in her diary to
allow that. The person who does feature as a particularly
rounded character in the whole story is Anne Frank herself,
with her longing for emotion and her inner conflicts. She won
both battles, for Peter and for herself. She won almost all the
battles that mattered to her—all but one, the most important
battle of all.

# 13 The Helpers

And what about the people who looked after the eight Jews in the Secret Annex for more than two years, doing all they could to help them, cheering them up, comforting them, always there? What made them risk their lives for fellow human beings at a time when others were ready to take the money offered for the betrayal of Jews in hiding?

I found a reproduction of an official form of the time, in German, in a book by Jacques Presser: it records the "delivery" by a Dutch citizen of five Jews—a family with three children aged eleven, fourteen, and seventeen—at the Jewish Emigration Center. The bottom part of the form consists of a pre-printed receipt: "I acknowledge receipt of 37.50 guilders from the Amsterdam branch office of the B.d.S. This sum is advanced from Jewish funds."[52]

The four helpers closest to the Jews in the Secret Annex had all been employees of Otto Frank's firm for several years; they were Miep Gies, Bep Voskuijl, Victor Kugler, and Johannes Kleiman. There was also Jan Gies, whom Miep had married in 1941.

It is impossible to establish now exactly what part each of

them played in caring for those in hiding. The only documentary evidence on the subject is in Anne's diaries. It is possible, of course, to count the number of times the names of the various helpers appear, but that merely enables us to draw conclusions about the way in which Anne herself saw the person concerned, not how much he or she really did individually. The order in which I describe the helpers, therefore, is not meant to suggest any priority.

## Victor Kugler, born in Hohenelbe, Austria, in 1900

He was Austrian by birth but became a Dutch citizen in 1938. Miep describes him as a "husky, good-looking man, dark-haired and precise," always formal and serious, a man who went about his work industriously.[53] He had been with the firm almost from the time it was founded and was Otto Frank's right-hand man. Later, when van Pels joined the company, he and van Pels worked very closely together. He was married and had no children. Miep emphasizes that he was fair to the company's other employees, but otherwise rather rigid in his views.

Kugler played an important part in the story of the Prinsengracht building, for in addition to his responsibility for the occupants of the Annex, he and Kleiman had to keep the firm going. Obviously much of the organization depended on him, and he seems to have given a great deal of thought to the safety of the people in hiding. For instance, he had a movable bookcase fitted in front of the door to the Secret Annex; it could be locked in place by a concealed hook, and it hid the door from the eyes of the wrong people. (The storeroom workers were not told about the Jews in hiding, and there

108    were constant visitors to the building: customers, the cleaning woman, the tax adviser, and so forth.)

Anne Frank gives little personal information about Victor Kugler. However, over time, he cannot have continued to be as stiff and formal as Miep describes him at first, for Anne says on August 5, 1943, that at lunchtime *Mr. Kugler hurries up the stairs* [. . .] *and comes in either wringing his hands or rubbing them in glee, depending on whether he's quiet and in a bad mood or talkative and in a good mood.*

He was a kindly, helpful man who brought her the magazine *Cinema & Theatre* every Monday; it was a source of great pleasure to her, interested as she was in film stars and the cinema. She mentions in passing, on April 18, 1944, that he remembered the rest of them too: *Mr. Kugler is supplying us with more and more newspapers.* Another and equally casual remark suggests that there were quite often differences of opinion on business matters between Kugler and van Pels. In the story "Freedom in the Secret Annex" (in the diary), Anne writes: *He* [van Pels] *must have worked himself into a rage again because of some blunder on Mr. Kugler's part.*

Kugler took a great deal of the responsibility for the people in hiding, as Anne Frank herself confirms. On May 26, 1944, she notes: *Miep and Mr. Kugler bear the greatest burden for us, and for all those in hiding—Miep in everything she does and Mr. Kugler through his enormous responsibility for the eight of us, which is sometimes so overwhelming that he can hardly speak from the pent-up tension and strain.*

This is a rather surprising remark. A man who could hardly speak for his pent-up tension and strain? None of the others seems to have reacted so emotionally to the pressures and anxieties. Thinking about it, I hit on a curious fact: Kugler's wife is not mentioned anywhere in the diary. Even Miep says only that after escaping from the camp where he was interned after arrest, he lived in his own apartment until the liberation of the Netherlands, and his wife looked after him. On the other hand, Ernst Schnabel in his book on Anne Frank mentions a letter in which Kugler apparently told the following story: "My wife and I visited the Franks once again in their flat in the Merwedeplein before they went into hiding. There were other friends there too. At supper Anne and my wife, who got on well with each other, were sitting side by side talking animatedly. Then the soup was served. Anne happened to be telling my wife something. Suddenly she stopped and looked my wife in the eyes, in silence, and my wife let her own spoon sink and looked at Anne in silence, and this went on between the two of them for some time. They just looked at each other in silence, until Anne suddenly glanced round at the rest of us and said out loud, 'There now, Mrs. Kraler [Kugler] and I have been talking to each other and nobody heard a word . . .' "[54]

This is a charming story, and one can easily imagine Anne acting like that. But if she and Kugler's wife got on so well together, why did he never tell the Franks anything about her while they were in hiding? If he had spoken about her often, Anne would surely have mentioned it at some point in the diary. Did he keep the presence of the Jews in hiding behind his firm's offices a secret from his wife? And if so, why? For fear of causing her anxiety? So as not to endanger her by making her an accomplice?

It is hard even to imagine someone risking his life throughout the working day and never mentioning it at home. Such a split in anyone's existence strikes me as almost unendurable.

110    If Kugler was really unable to talk to his wife about the difficult, dangerous situation in the Prinsengracht, if he had to be
constantly on his guard against saying anything that might
give him away, then the strain on him must have become
greater and greater. That would explain the difference between the two entries of August 5, 1943 (when Kugler is
likely to come hurrying up the stairs, talkative and in a good
mood), and May 26, 1944 (when he could sometimes scarcely
speak for the pent-up tension and strain).

Kugler was afraid. He was always conscious of the danger
threatening him and the rest of them. We can deduce as much
from the trouble he took to ensure that the people in hiding
were not reckless. If they committed some "blunder" he
would lose his temper and say so—surely a sign of suppressed anxiety in such a formal and courteous man. His constant helpfulness is all the more admirable. No one ever
seems to have questioned his loyalty, neither he himself nor
any of the others. We cannot know just why he helped them,
but he does not seem to have been a close personal friend,
like Kleiman or Miep and Jan Gies; social contact between the
Franks and the Kuglers was formal rather than intimate. I assume that Victor Kugler was a sympathetic, kindhearted man
who would not let down anyone in trouble even if it put him
under the utmost psychological strain.

### Johannes Kleiman, born in Koog an der Zaan, the Netherlands, in 1896

Kleiman was a close friend of the Franks and had known Otto
Frank ever since he first visited Amsterdam and tried to
found a branch of his father's bank there. Kleiman had done

Otto Frank's accounts even before he joined the firm on a permanent basis, at about the same time as van Pels.

Miep describes him as a middle-aged man of frail appearance, pale with delicate features, wearing glasses with large, thick lenses perched on his thin, pinched nose. She immediately liked and trusted him, and her relationship with him was a warm one.[55] Miep learned from Otto Frank that the idea of the hiding place had come from Kleiman.

Kleiman was always there when he was needed. It was he, for example, who met Pfeffer at the appointed place and took him to the Secret Annex. Otto Frank discussed business problems with him. Again, it was Kleiman who sold clothing and items of value such as Mrs. van Pels's fur coat when money began to run out. He got new pillows for Peter's sofa bed, borrowed girls' books for Anne, and bought his friends a little radio set so that they were not absolutely cut off from the world when the larger radio from Otto Frank's office had to be handed in. He sprinkled flea powder when the Secret Annex had a plague of fleas, and was helpful in planning small surprises for birthdays or Christmas.* He brought news of the outside world into the Secret Annex and discussed political events with its occupants. This was important in view of the lack of variety in their lives.

He seems to have been the most successful of the helpers in distracting and cheering his friends in hiding. He entertained them with jokes, brought them little presents and candy, and generally raised their spirits. Miep writes, "He'd leave his

---

* The Franks and many other Jewish families of the time participated in some of the customs of Christmas and other Christian holidays.

112   troubles behind him when he closed the swinging bookcase. He brought with him only strength, encouragement, and the ability to make all our friends feel so much better and brighter than he'd found them."[56] Anne herself calls him *unfailingly cheerful*, and writes in her diary for September 10, 1943: *"When Mr. Kleiman enters a room, the sun begins to shine," Mother said recently, and she's absolutely right.*

No wonder they all liked him. A little cheerfulness brought life into the place, and man does not live by bread alone. But Kleiman's health was poor—a source of concern to his friends in hiding. He had frequent internal stomach bleeding, which often kept him at home. One-fifth of Anne's remarks about him in her diary are about his health. How did he manage to remain so *cheerful and amazingly brave* and convey a sense of confidence, in spite of the recurrent stomach bleeding that sometimes even left him unconscious? Johannes Kleiman had a family: a wife and daughter. His wife knew what was going on from the first, and she too visited the Jews in hiding. Anne mentions her visits twice. Once indirectly, on December 24, 1943: *I'm . . . "in the depths of despair"* when, for example, Mrs. Kleiman comes by and talks about Jopie's hockey club, canoe trips, school plays and afternoon teas with friends. And a second time more directly, on May 31, 1944: *Mrs. Kleiman came for a visit in the afternoon and told us a lot about Jopie.* Kleiman himself later told Ernst Schnabel he was lucky to have a wife who did not complain. She must, however, have felt anxious about his health.[57]

Johannes Kleiman must have found it very helpful to have someone with whom he could discuss his fears. And he must have been badly afraid, even though he was obviously very successful in concealing the fact from his friends in hiding.

Anne at least noticed nothing. His frequent stomach bleeding
was probably due at least partly to the massive psychological
burdens he had to bear. A brave and cheering soul.

## Elisabeth Voskuijl, known as Bep, born around 1919 in the Netherlands

She joined Otto Frank's firm in 1937, to work in the office.
Miep describes her as a dark blonde, tall and very shy.[58] The
two young women liked each other at once and became
friends. At a later date Bep's father took a job in the storerooms.

Bep helped Miep with the shopping; Anne mentions, for instance, exercise books and new skirts bought for them by
Bep. Once she brought a picture postcard of the whole Dutch
royal family for Anne. (Juliane looked very young, said Anne,
so did the Queen, and the three little girls were adorable.
She thought it was *very nice* of Bep.) Another time, for no particular reason, Bep brought flowers when she came—three
bunches of narcissi and some grape hyacinths for Anne.

Anne and Bep probably had many conversations about film
stars. Bep liked going to the movies and would always tell
Anne in advance what film she was going to see on Saturday.
Anne would immediately tell her about the leading actors and
the reviews of the film. Miep says that Anne used to talk
about movies and movie stars to anyone who would listen. It
is curious, when you think about it, that her own writing was
so realistic, with none of the cloying romanticism in which a
film fan might have indulged.

Anne had a more direct, relaxed relationship with Bep than
with the other helpers; she mentions her more frequently,
perhaps because Bep was a good deal younger than any of the

114    other adults—about ten years younger than Miep. Anne liked Bep and was unhappy when her little sister had diphtheria and she had to stay at home in quarantine for several weeks.

Anne mentions Bep's feelings more than those of any of the other helpers. On October 9, 1942, she writes: *Bep is also very subdued. Her boyfriend is being sent to Germany.* Elsewhere, she describes how she and Bep winked at each other when Mrs. van Pels began on another long list of wishes. It sounds as if they were on the same wavelength, almost accomplices.

On September 29, 1943, Anne writes that Bep had had a "nervous fit" because she had so many things to do, and people kept complaining about the way she did them. *And when you think that she has her regular office work to do, that Mr. Kleiman is sick, that Miep is home with a cold and that Bep herself has a sprained ankle, boyfriend troubles and a grouchy father, it's no wonder she's at the end of her tether.* Anne seldom thought up so many excuses for someone else's bad temper.

The entry of March 2, 1944, makes Anne's sense of solidarity with Bep particularly clear. Bep had told Mrs. Frank and Mrs. van Pels how discouraged she was feeling. *What help did those two offer her? Our tactless mother, especially, only made things go from bad to worse. Do you know what her advice was? That she should think about all the other people in the world who are suffering! How can thinking about the misery of others help if you're miserable yourself? I said as much. Their response, of course, was that I should stay out of conversations of this sort. The grown-ups are such idiots! As if Peter, Margot, Bep and I didn't all have the same feelings.*

Clearly she regarded Bep as one of the young people rather than a grown-up, and sympathized with her problems. On May 25, 1944, there is a long passage in which Anne refers to

Bep and her fiancé and wonders whether they really ought to
marry. She does not think the young man good enough for
Bep—and argues her point with some arrogance, as a girl
from a prosperous, educated background herself.

Bep Voskuijl's situation was more complicated than it
might seem at first glance, for one of her sisters was involved
with an SS man.[59] However, she obviously did not suffer from
stress and the threat of outside circumstances as much as the
others. She was still young and relatively carefree. She seems
to have felt less anxiety than the rest about the possible consequences of what she was doing. To Anne, that in itself made
her an important member of the little band of helpers. In her
account of dinner in the Annex, she writes of Bep Voskuijl:
*Number nine is not part of our Annex family, although she does
share our house and table. Bep has a healthy appetite. She cleans
her plate and isn't choosy. Bep's easy to please and that pleases
us. She can be characterized as follows: cheerful, good-humored,
kind and willing.*

One helper whose services to the Jews in hiding are often
overlooked was Bep's father, Mr. Voskuijl, who worked in the
firm's storerooms until he fell ill. At first he knew nothing
about the people in hiding, but then he was told and, as Anne
puts it, was *helpfulness itself.* At Kugler's request he built the
movable bookcase and gave the inhabitants of the Secret Annex things he had made himself. Anne was very sorry for him
when he became ill, and felt angry with the doctors who told
him he had inoperable cancer. Her entry for June 15, 1943,
reads: *Now the good man can no longer let us know what's being
said and done in the warehouse, which is a disaster for us. Mr.
Voskuijl was our greatest source of help and support when it
came to safety measures. We miss him very much.*

116     Mr. Voskuijl too, by the standards of the time a very ordinary kind of man, seems to have reacted with the utmost helpfulness to the presence of the eight Jews hiding in the Secret Annex, even though by helping them he was putting himself in danger: that was not by any means an "ordinary" reaction.

## Miep Gies, born in Vienna, Austria, in 1909

Miep Santrouschitz, as she was before her marriage, was originally from Austria, like Victor Kugler. After the First World War an aid program for children in need arranged for her to go to foster parents in the Netherlands and recover her health, and she stayed there. She was a rather small woman, pretty, with a great interest in elegant clothes. As she herself says, she loved dancing; she was naturally energetic and a born organizer. She too had been employed by Otto Frank for some time and had joined the firm soon after Kugler, to work in the office.

Jan Gies, whom she married in 1941, had also become a friend of the Frank family through Miep. He was a social worker employed by the city of Amsterdam. After 1940, when Otto Frank foresaw that the Dutch economy would be "de-Judaized" and took the precaution of "Aryanizing" his firm, Jan Gies became its ostensible owner, together with Victor Kugler and Johannes Kleiman. Jan was tall, well dressed, and a few years older than Miep. She found him extremely attractive with his thick, fair hair and his warm eyes that sparkled with life.

Miep admired Otto Frank and his friendly if reserved nature, and over the years she became a real family friend. It was not surprising that when the call-up notice came for Margot, she and her husband were asked to help with preparations for the Franks to go into hiding. Later on, when one or another of the helpers was asked to spend the night in the Annex, probably because the children wanted some variety, the visitors were usually Miep and Jan. It was Miep who found Pfeffer, the eighth occupant of the Annex, and who kept him and Charlotte Kaletta in touch by letter. And naturally it was Miep and Jan who came to the Secret Annex when there had been a burglary in the building and soothed the alarmed occupants.

While Jan Gies kept up the spirits of the Jews in hiding with his often amusing stories, Miep saw to the more practical tasks, although according to Anne she also liked telling stories. She and Bep would prepare little surprises for birthdays and for Christmas, which the Franks and their friends in hiding celebrated together for the first time in 1942. She bought shoes for Anne and a banned book about Mussolini for Pfeffer, and when one of the cats was sick she took it to the vet. She brought a cake at Christmas and raisin bread for Pentecost, a holiday after Easter. Miep loved little surprises. (As provisions became increasingly short, of course the presents were smaller too.)

Above all, however, Miep was responsible for buying food. Anne's entry for July 11, 1943, is typical: *Miep has so much to carry she looks like a pack mule. She goes forth nearly every day to scrounge up vegetables, and then bicycles back with her purchases in large shopping bags. She's also the one who brings five library books with her every Saturday.*

The image of Miep as a *pack mule* is reinforced in her book *Anne Frank Remembered*, where she gives a detailed account of the difficulties of finding food for eight people every day, on top of her own requirements. In fact, she really had to find food for nine, since Miep and Jan Gies had an additional bur-

118   den: in the spring of 1943 they took in a young man who had
refused to sign the oath of loyalty demanded from university
students by the Germans, and who therefore had to go into
hiding. Miep and Jan did not mention their new, private pro-
tégé to their friends in the Secret Annex, because it would
have made them anxious. Nor did they mention that Jan became an active member of a resistance group in 1943.

Miep obviously tried not to think about the dangers sur-
rounding them, particularly as she saw no opportunity to discuss her fears with anyone. She writes, "Worst of all, when I
felt particularly weak, there was no one I could talk to about
my insecurities. Naturally, I couldn't speak of them to those
closest to me, Mr. and Mrs. Frank, nor could I speak of them
to Jo Kleiman, with whom I talked most often at the office. I
could not even speak of them to Jan. Jan was doing his own
illegal work, and I couldn't burden him further."[60]

Miep was the pack mule in a figurative sense too. She tried
not to sink into gloom and anxiety; she went on functioning.

Shopping then was not what it is today. You couldn't buy
everything at one big grocery store. Moreover, food was ra-
tioned; since 1941, coupons had been handed out on presen-
tation of a card stating that you were a regular customer of a
shop. Jan had connections with underground resistance
workers, so it was possible for the people hiding in the Secret
Annex to buy forged or stolen ration cards on the black mar-
ket, but not eight cards; that would have been too expensive.
It is also hard to imagine the sheer amount of time Miep had
to spend shopping for food every day. Luckily, she could at
least get bread from an acquaintance of Kleiman and meat
from a butcher whom van Pels knew. A "vegetable man" mentioned several times by Anne in the diary was helpful too, and

did not ask unnecessary questions. As time went on, however, food supplies in the occupied Netherlands were harder and harder to find, and Miep had to visit more and more shops to get anything at all. But the terrible Hunger Winter, when many thousands of people starved to death, was not until the winter of 1944–45, and by then the Franks and their friends were no longer hiding in the Secret Annex.

Miep went shopping, and coped, and fetched and carried, and worked. In spite of all her troubles she, like the other helpers, tried to show a cheerful face to the Jews in hiding. The friendship that already existed between her and the Franks became even deeper. Only once, on May 26, 1944, does Anne Frank speak of any misunderstanding between her and those she was protecting: *Miep came up one afternoon all flushed and asked Father straight out if we thought they too were infected with the current anti-Semitism. Father was stunned and quickly talked her out of the idea, but some of Miep's suspicion has lingered on. They're doing more errands for us now and showing more of an interest in our troubles, though we certainly shouldn't bother them with our woes. Oh, they're such good, noble people!* Unfortunately we do not know what led up to this incident, but the mere fact that Miep felt she might be suspected of anti-Semitism shows how poisonous the general atmosphere was during the occupation and how insidiously distrust could spread, even among close friends.

Evidence that Miep was anything but anti-Semitic can be seen in her reaction to the Franks' plans to go into hiding. It would have been in the spring of 1942, she says, that Otto Frank told her about his plan to hide in the annex behind the office building with his wife and daughters and the van Pels family. He asked if she had any objections. No, she said, none.

**120**   Then he asked if she would be prepared to take the responsibility of providing for them when they were in hiding. Miep answered with a simple "Of course."[61] She added no ifs or buts.

However, her willingness to help could by no means be expected. Christians and Jews were forbidden to have anything to do with each other, and the Germans had made it very clear indeed to the Dutch population that anyone helping Jews in any way whatever must expect severe punishment— even, in some circumstances, the death sentence.

"Of course," she said, and she kept her word. She will probably never cease to grieve that despite all her efforts, she could not save those eight people.

I wonder whether relations between the helpers and the people in hiding were really as serene as they sound. Sometimes they must all have felt angry and irritated—the hidden Jews because they were dependent on the helpers, the helpers because those they were helping made their lives even more difficult. They must have felt as if they were chained to one another without any chance of release and with no end in sight.

If the helpers had wished to be free at last of the anxiety of their burden, that would be only too easy to understand. However, such a wish was never expressed, any more than the Jews in hiding indulged in reproaches or accusations. I find it hard to imagine how they (or at least the adults) coped with being constantly dependent on the goodwill of others. For all the gratitude they naturally felt, they must have had mixed feelings at least at times. But presumably their acute danger weighed so heavily on them that there was simply no room left for aggression, the inevitable result of dependency in any relationship. Perhaps it is essential to suppress anger or even mild annoyance with people if your whole life depends on their help. Anything else would be too risky. Conversely, the helpers could hardly afford to feel aggressive toward the people in their care, or the whole structure they had erected to repress their fear would have collapsed. Any unconscious aggression may have been vented but also checked by relating stories of the terrible fate of other Jews who had no one to help them.

The people in hiding did their best not to be a burden to the helpers, but it was useless. They *were* a burden. However, both parties, those in hiding and their helpers, obviously had a firmly established set of moral values and a strong sense of self-discipline. When you had made a promise you kept it. All concerned could be sure of that. In the circumstances, this was essential for survival.

On August 4, 1944, Kugler and Kleiman were arrested with the eight people in the Secret Annex. The two women, Miep and Bep, were not detained. Obviously it was thought that they had not been involved in the "crime" of hiding Jews. Kugler and Kleiman were taken to a remand prison. No legal proceedings were brought against them. On September 18, Kleiman, suffering from stomach bleeding again, was released for health reasons through the intervention of the Red Cross. A week later he went back to work in the Prinsengracht building and, with the assistance of Miep and Bep, continued to run the firm until the end of the war. Kugler was sent from prison to a labor camp. He and six hundred other men recruited for forced labor were to be marched to Germany on March 28, 1945, but just before reaching the border they

122　came under fire from British troops, and, in the ensuing confusion, Kugler managed to escape. He made his way to Amsterdam and hid with his wife until the end of the war.[62]

Four of the helpers are now dead. Kleiman died in Amsterdam in 1959. Kugler emigrated to Canada in 1955 and died in Toronto in 1981. Bep Wijk-Voskuijl died in Amsterdam in 1983. Jan Gies died in 1993. Only Miep is still alive, living in Amsterdam.

Five people were prepared to take responsibility for the lives of others at a time when inhumanity was the general rule. Not just that, they did it as something perfectly natural and made great efforts to show a cheerful face to the people they were helping and to hide their own frequent anxieties.

Anne Frank did not think about the dangers to which the helpers were exposed very often, but she was aware of them. On January 28, 1944, she expresses her gratitude in her diary:

*The best example of this is our own helpers, who have managed to pull us through so far and will hopefully bring us safely to shore, because otherwise they'll find themselves sharing the fate of those they're trying to protect. Never have they uttered a single word about the burden we must be, never have they complained that we're too much trouble. They come upstairs every day and talk to the men about business and politics, to the women about food and wartime difficulties and to the children about books and newspapers. They put on their most cheerful expressions, bring flowers and gifts for birthdays and holidays and are always ready to do what they can. That's something we should never forget; while others display their heroism in battle or against the Germans, our helpers prove theirs every day by their good spirits and affection.*

# The Secret Annex and the Outside World

## "I KNOW WE CAN'T LEAVE HERE"

Today we are used to seeing the events of the Second World War in retrospect, beginning from the end of it. For instance, when we hear of the Germans' "successful Russian campaign" we know that it only seemed successful at first. In July 1942, when the Frank family went into hiding in the Secret Annex, it looked as if the Germans were going to win the war. In August 1942, when Anne Frank wrote her first letters to Kitty, the German Sixth Army reached Stalingrad, a major industrial city on the Volga, where it was surrounded by Soviet troops. At the time no one could have imagined that this incident would ultimately lead to the defeat of Germany in the Second World War. Anne Frank also misinterpreted Stalingrad as a case of heroic but doomed Soviet resistance to the Germans. She was convinced that the city would fall in the end; that is the way to read her diary entry of November 9, 1942: *Stalingrad, the Russian city that has been under attack for three months, still hasn't fallen into German hands.*

The Third Reich was still at the height of its power. Its rise had begun in 1933, when Adolf Hitler was appointed Reich Chancellor. It is usually and misleadingly said that Hitler

124   "seized power," but that phrase veils the truth. Hindenburg certainly appointed Hitler to the post of Chancellor, but the National Socialists had already proved the strongest party in the parliamentary elections of July 1932, and when new elections were held on March 5, 1933, they won 43.9 percent of the vote. It can hardly be said, then, that Hitler seized power. He demanded power, and millions of Germans handed it to him.

Yet he had already and quite clearly stated his main intentions in 1925 in his book *Mein Kampf.* By 1939 five and a half million copies of the book had been distributed in Germany. Hitler's aims were:

> 1. To conquer new *Lebensraum* (living space) for the German people in the east, which led to the Second World War.
> 2. To destroy the Jews of Europe, which led to the creation of concentration camps such as Auschwitz, Chelmno (Kulmhof), Majdanek, Belzec, Sobibor, and Treblinka.

When the Frank and van Pels families and Mr. Pfeffer moved into the Secret Annex, the Wannsee Conference on what the Nazis called the "final solution of the Jewish problem" had already taken place. The decision to exterminate all European Jews was decided there on January 20, 1942. Hundreds of thousands had already been deported to concentration camps. Hundreds of thousands had fallen victim to the massacres and mass shootings carried out by the *Einsatzgruppen** (for

---

* *Einsatzgruppen:* special military units created to hunt down Jews and opponents of National Socialism, operating in most of the areas occupied by German troops, in particular in Poland and the USSR; the number of people murdered by these units is estimated to have been two million.[63]

instance, the number of victims in Kiev in September 1941 **125** was 34,000, in Riga in December 1941 27,000, and in Vilna 32,000). The first experimental gassings took place at Auschwitz in September 1941.[64] The death factories had already been built at Chelmno, Majdanek, Treblinka, Belzec, Sobibor, and Auschwitz. The first gassing of prisoners who could no longer work was carried out at Auschwitz on May 4, 1942; it was kept strictly secret.[65]

The "resettlement" of Jews in the east, a euphemistic name for deportations, was going ahead; the annihilation of the Jewish population of Europe had begun.

The state of the Netherlands was also affected, to an extent made clear from a letter sent to Heinrich Himmler, SS Reich Leader and head of the German police. The letter was from the Higher SS Commander and Chief of Police with the Office of the Reich Commissar for the occupied Netherlands area:

The Hague, 14 Sept. 1942
Confidential

Subject: Deportation of Jews

Reich Leader,
I have the pleasure of making you an interim report on the deportation of the Jews. To date we have marched 20,000 Jews to Auschwitz, those intended for punitive deportation being assigned to Mauthausen. Holland contains some 120,000 Jews in all for deportation, although this figure also includes those of mixed race, who will remain here for the time being. By agreement with the Reich Commissar, however, I am deporting all Jewish partners in mixed marriages where there are no children of such marriages. This will amount to

some 6,000 cases, so that for the time being 14,000 Jews of
mixed marriages will remain here. [. . .] The new units of Dutch
police are performing extremely well in the matter of the
Jewish question and are arresting hundreds of Jews both
day and night. The only danger is that occasionally a member
of the police puts his own hand in the till to enrich himself
with Jewish property.[66]

Twenty thousand Jews, then, had already been "marched" to
Auschwitz or "deported" to labor camps.

The Dutch population did not know what was going on in
these camps, although in the United Kingdom the BBC reported gassings in Poland as early as June 1942.[67] These
reports were probably assumed by most people to be rumors
or counterpropaganda; according to Anne, for instance, Jan
Gies still thought on February 3, 1944, that *the British and
the Russians are probably exaggerating for propaganda purposes,
just like the Germans.* How could any normal human being
even imagine such an inhuman, bureaucratically planned
program of genocide? But the history of the Third Reich
has shown that reality can outstrip the imagination in its
horror.

The Frank and van Pels families and Pfeffer had some idea
of the gravity of their situation, or at least the adults did, but
they did not know how bad it really was. They sensed, however, that they must not fall into the hands of the Germans,
and feared it so much that they would even allow themselves
to put their helpers in danger. There are accounts of Jews who
declined to go into hiding because they did not want to risk
the lives of others. Most of them paid for their scruples with
their lives.

The eight people in hiding lived behind drawn curtains.
Out of necessity, their whole world was the Secret Annex.
What happened there? What went on in that building from
July 5, 1942, until August 4, 1944?

The answer is simple: very little. Notable events were few
and far between. Pfeffer moved in. Number 263 Prinsengracht was acquired by a new owner, who visited the building
with an architect, but Kleiman managed to divert him from
the Secret Annex with an excuse and luckily he did not come
back. There was a burglary on July 16, 1943 (the most valuable items stolen were the coupons for 330 pounds of sugar);
another burglary on March 1, 1944; and finally a third on
April 11, 1944, which made the hidden occupants of the Annex terrified that they might be found. Everything else was
more or less humdrum in the secret rooms. The safety of the
Annex residents depended on a lack of activity. Any loud
noise, particularly during the day when there were workers
on the floors below, would mean exposure and possible cap-
ture. And for two years, their dramas were small: sometimes
the toilet was blocked, or the cat brought fleas in, or they
thought they heard a burglar, or someone was sick.

But illness could be a serious threat to people in hiding.
The eight inhabitants of the Secret Annex were lucky: none of
them fell seriously ill, although they sometimes suffered from
coughs (and they feared coughing in particular because it
might be heard outside). For Jews in hiding and their helpers,
it was vitally important to stay healthy. Appendicitis could
mean death, and unfortunately such incidents were common
enough. The death of a person in hiding confronted his
helpers with almost insoluble problems. There are reports of
the dead being thrown into canals or secretly buried in front

128    gardens. Discussion of this problem must have been taboo. Even thinking about it was probably avoided.

So not much happened in the Secret Annex, but there were still difficult situations, for those in hiding were not spared the effects of the war. Quite apart from the constantly deteriorating food supply, they all suffered stress from Allied air raids on military targets and German positions in the Netherlands. They worried that the bombs would miss their intended targets, destroying homes and hiding places. When Allied aircraft flew over the Netherlands toward Germany, they came under fire from German antiaircraft systems. The threat of a plane crashing on the Annex was also very real. After 1942 the British carried out more and more air raids by night on cities in the north and west of Germany, particularly the industrial centers of the Rhineland and the Ruhr, and after January 1943, American bombers also carried out daytime raids.

Anne mentions the destruction of the Carlton Hotel when a British plane came down on it on April 27, 1943. The whole corner of Vijzelstraat and Singel burned down; it was only a few hundred yards from the Secret Annex. North Amsterdam was bombed on July 19, and Anne mentions two hundred dead and countless wounded. A week later she records a particularly bad day. There had been air raid warnings even in the morning, and around two in the afternoon Amsterdam harbor, about one mile away from the Secret Annex, was bombed. *The house shook and the bombs kept falling. I was clutching my "escape bag," more because I wanted to have something to hold on to than because I wanted to run away. I know we can't leave here, but if we had to, being seen on the streets would be just as dangerous as getting caught in an air raid.*

There were air raid warnings at supper, when they were doing the washing-up, and again at one-thirty in the morning.
Every warning must have struck panic into the occupants of
the Secret Annex, who could not take shelter in a cellar or
a bunker. Any threatening sound heard outside—gunfire,
sirens, the drone of aircraft—brought the dangers of their situation home to them, and to make matters even worse they
could not get any information for themselves. They were dependent on what they learned from their helpers—and, of
course, from the radio news.

Radio broadcasts were very important to the people in the
Secret Annex, particularly the news from the BBC and from
Radio Oranje, as a passage from Anne's entry for June 15,
1943, shows: *It's true: as the reports from outside grow worse
and worse, the radio, with its wondrous voice, helps us not to lose
heart and to keep telling ourselves, "Cheer up, keep your spirits
high, things are bound to get better!"*

In hiding, they got their information on the military situation from the radio, and the news naturally had a huge influence on their frame of mind. Anne notes on November 5,
1942: *The English have at last had a few successes in Africa, and
Stalingrad is still holding out too, so the gentlemen here are very
cheerful and this morning we had coffee and tea.* (This entry is
from version A.)

Although during 1943 it gradually began to seem possible
that the Germans might lose the war, the hidden occupants of
the Annex alternated between hope and doubt. Their depen-
dence on the news shows clearly in the frequency with which
Anne Frank speaks about the Allied invasion everyone longed
for (she mentions it twelve times in all). She very often mentions their feelings about it too.

February 27, 1943: *Pim is expecting the invasion any day now.*

August 18, 1943: [. . .] *Mrs. van Daan begins again: "The invasion seems as if it will never come!"*

February 3, 1944: *Invasion fever is mounting daily throughout the country. If you were here, I'm sure you'd be as impressed as I am at the many preparations, though you'd no doubt laugh at all the fuss we're making. Who knows, it may all be for nothing!* [. . .] *All day long that's all I hear. Invasion, invasion, nothing but invasion. Arguments about going hungry, dying, bombs, fire extinguishers, sleeping bags, identity cards, poison gas, etc., etc. Not exactly cheerful.*

May 3, 1944: *We're having a vacation from politics. There's nothing, and I mean absolutely nothing, to report. I'm also gradually starting to believe that the invasion will come. After all, they can't let the Russians do all the dirty work; actually, the Russians aren't doing anything at the moment either.*

May 22, 1944: *On May 20, Father lost his bet and had to give five jars of yogurt to Mrs. van Daan: the invasion still hasn't begun. I can safely say that all of Amsterdam, all of Holland, in fact the entire western coast of Europe, all the way down to Spain, are talking about the invasion day and night, debating, making bets and . . . hoping.*

And then at last, on June 6, 1944: *"This is D Day,"* the BBC announced at twelve. *"This is the day."* The invasion has begun!

The Secret Annex was in a state of great excitement for some time. *Our mood is rising,* says Anne, and *everything is going well.* In hiding, they hoped it would all soon be over. Anne even thought she might be able to go back to school in October. Her hopes rose even further when news of the attempt on Hitler's life became known on July 21, 1944. Anne's reactions are positively euphoric. *I'm finally getting optimistic. Now, at last, things are going well! They really are! Great news! An assassination attempt has been made on Hitler's life, and for once not by Jewish Communists or English capitalists, but by a German general who's not only a count, but young as well. The Führer owes his life to "Divine Providence": he escaped, unfortunately, with only a few minor burns and scratches.*

It is impossible to read these passages without a sense of grief and anguish. All Anne Frank's hopes were in vain. The liberation came too late for her.

# 15 Anne's Development in Hiding

## "THEN I'LL REALLY BE GROWN-UP"

Anne Frank was just thirteen years old when she went into hiding in the Secret Annex. She developed physically into a woman while she was there. It cannot have been easy for her, having no girlfriends around with whom she could talk and compare notes. She lacked the calming influence and sense of proportion that adolescent girls get from realizing they are not alone and that these profound changes are happening to other girls as well.

Of course Anne knew what her physical development meant, but there was no one she could talk to for whom it held the same importance. On October 3, 1942, she mentions a book she has been reading, and adds: *In addition, it mentions Eva's menstruation. Oh, I long to have my period—then I'll really be grown-up.* And on November 2, 1942, she writes to Kitty: *P.S. I forgot to mention the important news that I'm probably going to have my period soon. I can tell because I keep finding a whitish smear in my panties, and Mother predicted it would start soon. I can hardly wait. It's such a momentous event. Too bad I can't use sanitary napkins, but you can't get them anymore, and Mummy's tampons can be used only by women who've had a baby.*

We can conclude from the (misinformed) mention of tampons that she had already talked to her mother or Margot about menstruation; there are no other indications later. She seems to have felt more embarrassment on the subject as time went by: a year later, reading through her diary, she was obviously quite shocked by her ingenuous remarks here. On January 22, 1944, she added a comment to this earlier postscript: *I wouldn't be able to write that kind of thing anymore. [. . .] It embarrasses me greatly to read the pages dealing with subjects that I remembered as being nicer than they actually were. My descriptions are so indelicate. But enough of that.*

However, on October 10, 1942, a week after she first mentioned the subject of menstruation, she had not yet lost her freedom from embarrassment: *My vagina is getting wider all the time, but I could also be imagining it. When I'm on the w.c. I sometimes look then I can see quite definitely that the urine comes out of a little hole in the vagina, but above it there is something else, there is a hole in that too, but I don't know what for.*[68] (This entry is from version A.) Writing so frankly in a diary is most unusual and says a good deal about Anne's straightforward approach at the time. Later she returns to the subject of self-examination only once, describing the external female genitals, but compared with this earlier entry the passage is more impersonal and general and gives only an indirect idea of the great interest Anne was taking in her own body.

There is no mention of Anne's first period (although there may have been an entry about it in the lost 1943 diary). She says almost in passing, on January 6, 1944, that she has already had her period three times. She feels grown-up now and mentions the subject only once again, on May 3, 1944: *I hadn't had my period for more than two months, but it finally*

134  *started last Sunday. Despite the mess and bother, I'm glad it
hasn't deserted me.*

By now she had developed a very acute sense of modesty
even in relation to her family—an indication of the way she
was withdrawing into herself. On January 6, 1944, she writes:
*I'm not prudish, Kitty, and yet every time they give a blow-by-
blow account of their trips to the bathroom, which they often do,
my whole body rises in revolt.* She found her body, with all its
changes and new reactions, mysterious and not something to
be taken for granted, so any reference to the less dignified
physical functions seemed to her almost like sacrilege.

How much did Anne know about the facts of life? Certainly
not enough, and probably only through elaborate circumlocu-
tions, since when Peter showed her *the male sexual organs* on
one of the cats in the building she summoned up all her
courage and asked what they were called. Peter obviously did
not know either, and Anne comments: *How are we supposed to
know these words? Most of the time you just come across them by
accident.* (It is doubtful whether Peter knew the facts of life
either. In discussing birth control he coined his own German
word, *Präsentivmittel,* which should really have been *Präser-
vativmittel,* meaning condoms. However, it is possible that
Anne herself did not understand him correctly and was the
one who got the word wrong.)

Anne Frank had entered the Secret Annex at the age of thirteen, when she was still a child, at least physically. At the
time of her arrest on August 4, 1944, she was fifteen, and no
longer a child, but a woman.

She had, of course, developed mentally and intellectually as
well as physically during her time in hiding. The extreme situation in which she found herself meant more than the re-

striction of her movements; it also represented a challenge to a young girl firmly determined not to resign herself to her fate. In a sense the situation gave Anne a chance to get to know herself.

When the family first went into hiding, she felt it was very exciting, an adventure. That reaction would have been partly because of her age, but it also indicates one way in which she would develop: she was not about to give in. Grief and anger never lasted long with her before she felt the need for cheerfulness again, and if real life did not offer it she would create it for herself. She had the gift of making reality into a kind of dramatic performance in which she could participate as actor or spectator, and it was a gift she cultivated during her time in hiding. Examples range from her account of Dussel opening his dental practice (December 10, 1942), to the description of a suspected burglary (March 25, 1943) and her account of Mrs. van Pels's attempt to cut Peter's hair (May 11, 1944). In telling these stories she showed a great talent for drama and comedy, making an exciting story out of a real incident. I would really like to know whether she found the events dramatic and exciting at the time, or whether she added those qualities later when she wrote them up.

Her romantic feelings could be nourished by a minimum of reality too. She could experience no mild midsummer nights, mist rising from the canals, a darkening sky with light fading on the horizon, a sunset at sea—all she had was an attic with a dormer window through which she could see the tower of the Westerkerk (a church), the top of a chestnut tree, a bit of sky, a bird now and then, a cloud. She used these tiny snippets of nature to create a world that had little to do with reality as she knew it but that allowed her to experience inspiring ideas and emotions. The moon symbolized romantic longings to Anne, as to so many others. On June 13, 1944, she writes: *It's not just my imagination—looking at the sky, the clouds, the moon and the stars really does make me feel calm and hopeful. It's much better medicine than valerian or bromide. Nature makes me feel humble and ready to face every blow with courage!* This inspiring contemplation of the natural world is also found quite often in *Tales from the Secret Annex*—written by a girl who for two whole years could catch only a tiny glimpse of nature, surrounded by curtains and a window frame.

One source of Anne's ability to re-create reality was certainly her longing for happiness. In the story "Happiness"[69] we can see what the word meant to her:

> *One free afternoon, I went alone for a walk on the moor. I sat down and dreamed for a while. When I looked up again, I realized that it was a glorious day. Until then, I had been so wrapped up in my own gloomy thoughts that I had paid no attention to it. From the moment that I saw and felt the beauty all around me, that little nagging inner voice stopped reminding me of my worries. I could no longer think or feel anything but that this was beauty and this was truth. [. . .] Later I understood that, on that afternoon, I had for the first time found happiness within myself. I also realized that no matter what the circumstances, happiness is always there.*

Anne Frank wanted happiness, joy, a little cheerfulness, and she created all these for herself. No one in the Secret Annex handed cheerfulness to her on a plate. The adults were too in-

volved in their own fears and problems to offer Anne, who
hungered for happiness, what she needed.

One question has interested me ever since I first read the diary: How is it that Anne Frank does not seem at all religious at the start of the diary, but often refers to God at the end? How did the change come about? What idea had Anne formed of God?

Hanneli Goslar, Anne's childhood friend, tells us that "Mrs. Frank and Margot went to synagogue once in a while, but Anne and her father went much less frequently."[70] And elsewhere we are told that "she [Anne] followed in her father's footsteps and wasn't religious at all."[71]

The first mention of religion or God in the diary comes on October 29, 1942. Anne's father wanted her to know the German classics, and was planning to read them aloud to her in the evenings. Following his good example, Anne says, her mother pressed a prayer book into her hands and *I read a few prayers in German, just to be polite.* At this point she obviously had no interest in religion.

Up to November 1943 the word "God" appears only twice more; both passages are from version B, and were therefore written after Anne Frank's attitude toward God had changed.

On April 2, 1943, she mentions that the previous night, as she was lying in bed waiting for her father to tuck her in and say her prayers with her, her mother had come in and suggested the two of them say prayers together instead. These evening prayers were probably less a truly religious act than the custom, usual at the time, of parents saying a bedtime prayer with their children.

**138**     Anne Frank's idea of God changed in the autumn of 1943. It may help us to understand how and why if we look more closely at her fears. How frightened was she, and of what, and how did she cope with those fears?

When she first went into hiding Anne was afraid of discovery, no doubt because the adults in the Annex with her and their helpers kept insisting on the need for caution and kept these fears alive in thirteen-year-old Anne—if indeed they did not arouse them in the first place. It is easy to imagine what they said: Hush, Anne, no one must hear us! Anne, for God's sake leave that curtain alone—suppose someone saw you? Be careful, Anne, look out! And over and over again: If they hear us, if they find us, if, if . . .

Anne's reaction to such warnings is clear from her entry of July 11, 1942, in which she writes of listening to the radio: *Last night the four of us went down to the private office and listened to England on the radio. I was so scared someone might hear it that I literally begged Father to take me back upstairs. Mother understood my anxiety and went with me. Whatever we do, we're very afraid the neighbors might hear or see us.* Tuning in to the BBC and indeed any other broadcasts from "enemy transmitters" was of course forbidden.

Another fear keeps emerging in the diary: Anne was afraid of aircraft and gunfire. Her entry of March 10, 1943, is typical of her reactions: *We had a short circuit last night, and besides that, the guns were booming away until dawn. I still haven't got over my fear of planes and shooting, and I crawl into Father's bed nearly every night for comfort. I know it sounds childish, but wait till it happens to you! The ack-ack guns make so much noise you can't hear your own voice.* There are two elements to her fears in this passage: first, the threat from outside, the sound of cannon fire, cannot be drowned out; and second, she feels she is helpless in the face of danger. She reacts by taking refuge with her father, but not for protection as she would have done when younger; she knows now that comfort is all he can give her.

Both fears, the fear of discovery and the fear of gunfire, were based on reality; they emerge in certain situations and then go underground again.

A change comes in the entry of May 2, 1943, when Mr. van Pels said they would have to stay in the Secret Annex until the end of the year. Anne thought that was a long time, but it could be endured. And then we hear for the first time of her doubts that the "adventure" will have a happy ending. She sees the road lying ahead of her in dark tones: *But who can assure us that this war, which has caused nothing but pain and sorrow, will then be over? And that nothing will have happened to us and our helpers long before that time? No one! That's why each and every day is filled with tension. Expectation and hope generate tension, as does fear—for example, when we hear a noise inside or outside the house, when the guns go off or when we read new "proclamations" in the paper.*

She falls victim to these new, deeper fears and can find no way of freeing herself. On one occasion she says she was *petrified* when the others were wondering if they dared send her to an optician for the glasses she needed. And on September 16, she writes: *I've been taking valerian every day to fight the anxiety and depression, but it doesn't stop me from being even more miserable the next day.*

In the second half of 1943, her fears no longer derive solely from her situation in the Secret Annex; they become all-embracing, existential. Anne feels rejected by the world and wonders about the meaning of life. This change is particularly clear in her entries of October 29 and November 8, 1943, where her confinement has come to symbolize despair and vulnerability. She lies on the divan and sleeps, because *sleep makes the silence and the terrible fear go by more quickly, helps pass the time, since it's impossible to kill it.*

On November 8 Anne confesses that by now she cannot even imagine how the world around her can ever be normal again. She does talk, she says, about "after the war," but it's as if that were a castle in the air. She then finds a very dramatic and striking metaphor for her feelings:

> *I see the eight of us in the Annex as if we were a patch of blue sky surrounded by menacing black clouds. The perfectly round spot on which we're standing is still safe, but the clouds are moving in on us, and the ring between us and the approaching danger is being pulled tighter and tighter. We're surrounded by darkness and danger, and in our desperate search for a way out we keep bumping into each other. We look at the fighting down below and the peace and beauty up above. In the meantime, we've been cut off by the dark mass of clouds, so that we can go neither up nor down. It looms before us like an impenetrable wall, trying to crush us, but not yet able to. I can only cry out and implore, "Oh, ring, ring, open wide and let us out!"*

Deep despair, and still no God, but she is coming closer to such a concept. She can no longer endure her fear and vulnerability. Who else but God, who is responsible for everything, can give her the confidence that reality does not offer?

On November 27, 1943, Anne writes about praying for the

first time, and directly asks God to help her. From now on God and nature—seen as interchangeable—take on the function of comforting her, cheering her, and soothing her fears. She notes on January 30, 1944: *Last night I went downstairs in the dark, all by myself, after having been there with Father a few nights before. I stood at the top of the stairs while German planes flew back and forth, and I knew I was on my own, that I couldn't count on others for support. My fear vanished. I looked up at the sky and trusted in God.* She retained that trust. On February 23, 1944, she writes: *The best remedy for those who are frightened, lonely or unhappy is to go outside, somewhere they can be alone, alone with the sky, nature and God. For then and only then can you feel that everything is as it should be and that God wants people to be happy amid nature's beauty and simplicity.*

Her fears for her life as a whole are gone; only the concrete fears arising from the situation remain. Her story "Fear"[72] can be seen as the key to her own fears and the refuge she found in God and nature. Anne's first-person narrator looks back at a terrifying air raid that put her parents and brothers and sisters right out of her mind, so that she thinks only of herself and her need to get away. Suddenly she finds herself in a meadow, looking up at the sky, and realizes that she no longer feels afraid but at peace.

The idea of God also provided Anne Frank with a figure embodying the moral authority she would not allow in any human being. On July 6, 1944, she writes: *People who are religious should be glad, since not everyone is blessed with the ability to believe in a higher order. You don't even have to live in fear of eternal punishment; the concepts of purgatory, heaven and hell are difficult for many people to accept, yet religion itself, any re-*

*ligion, keeps a person on the right path. Not the fear of God, but upholding your own sense of honor and obeying your own conscience.*

Anne Frank needed someone to relieve her of her fears when they became unbearable, so that she could find her way back to herself. Some might say her faith in God was a child's whistling in the dark, but what if it was? She managed to find help in the most dangerous of circumstances.

I cannot help wondering what it was like for her later in Auschwitz, in Bergen-Belsen. Could she retain her belief in God there?

I would very much like to think so.

# 16 Anne's Problems with Herself

## "A BUNDLE OF CONTRADICTIONS"

We are used to thinking of Anne Frank as someone who matured early and was wise before her time. In reality, however, she probably presented a number of problems, particularly to herself. And she must often have been an uncomfortable companion for the others, with her keen powers of observation and her sharp tongue.

In the last entry, dated August 1, 1944, she writes: *As I've told you, what I say is not what I feel, which is why I have a reputation for being boy-crazy as well as a flirt, a smart aleck and a reader of romances. The happy-go-lucky Anne laughs, gives a flippant reply, shrugs her shoulders and pretends she doesn't give a darn.* That is how she seems on the outside, but inside, she says, she is quite different: *The quiet Anne reacts in just the opposite way. If I'm being completely honest, I'll have to admit that it does matter to me, that I'm trying very hard to change myself, but that I'm always up against a more powerful enemy.*

That more powerful enemy was not outside but inside Anne; she was struggling against herself. Her efforts to improve herself and bring out the good part of her character show that she did not feel naturally good. Even her struggle

**144** for strength must be seen in this light. She knew her failings and her weaknesses and fought against them. Her urge for self-education and self-perfection must have been encouraged by her father. As early as 1939 he had written in a letter that she later stuck into her diary: "I have often told you that you must educate yourself. We have agreed [on] the 'controls' with each other [. . .]."[73]

Her struggle for self-perfection, as recorded in the diary, begins on September 28, 1942, with Anne's admission to having *faults and shortcomings.* However, this point is made in self-defense and as yet leads nowhere.

Only two months later, on November 28, 1942, it is obvious that Anne is seriously anxious and confused about her many weaknesses: *In bed at night, as I ponder my many sins and exaggerated shortcomings, I get so confused by the sheer amount of things I have to consider that I either laugh or cry, depending on my mood. Then I fall asleep with the strange feeling of wanting to be different than I am or being different than I want to be, or perhaps of behaving differently than I am or want to be.*

Her constant fight against her shortcomings probably also prevented her from feeling much sympathy for the weaknesses of her companions in hiding. On March 7, 1944, she describes her struggles thus: *This left me on my own to face the difficult task of improving myself so I wouldn't have to hear their reproaches, because they made me so despondent.* And on June 13, 1944, she wrote: *I know my various faults and shortcomings better than anyone else, but there's one difference: I also know that I want to change, will change and already have changed greatly!*[74]

On July 6, 1944, she even offers a prescription for beginning and winning the fight against one's shortcomings and weaknesses of character. *How noble and good everyone could be if, at the end of each day, they were to review their own behavior and weigh up the rights and wrongs. They would automatically try to do better at the start of each new day and, after a while, would certainly accomplish a great deal. Everyone is welcome to this prescription; it costs nothing and is definitely useful. Those who don't know will have to find out by experience that "a quiet conscience gives you strength"!* I assume that she really did follow her own advice, that her strategy was to reconcile the outer Anne with the inner Anne by regularly giving her attention to the inner Anne once a day.

However it may sometimes seem, Anne did not want to improve herself just to please other people and turn into a good girl who would win approval. Her project of self-improvement was bound up with her hopes of giving some structure to her life and perhaps reconciling the inner contradictions that fretted her. Her whole development was influenced by this struggle with her own contradictory nature.

Anne had opposing sides to her personality. I do not mean that she was hesitant or uncertain, but there were two sides to her character and they were always in conflict. On the one hand she was a highly sensitive, thin-skinned girl; on the other she was precocious and mocking. On the one hand she had a very precise gift for observation and an acute mind; on the other she felt deep romantic longings. On the one hand she formed concrete ideas of an independent future in journalism; on the other she dreamed of marriage and children.

Her feelings and moods were marked by contrast and conflict, too; euphoric feelings coexisting with states of depression, a zest for life with anxiety, hope with resignation. Indeed, she actually called herself *a bundle of contradictions*.

146     I am very much aware of her contradictory character, but I
do not, like Anne herself, feel there was something sinister
about it. On the contrary, I am glad for her, because it enabled
her to express the riches of her inner nature. What I do admit
to finding rather hard to take is Anne's arrogance in making
her demands on life. She did not want one thing or the other;
she wanted both, and she felt superior to people who, as she
saw it, wanted less from life. On May 8, 1944, she writes: *I
can assure you, I'm not so set on a bourgeois life as Mother and
Margot. I'd like to spend a year in Paris and London learning the
languages and studying art history. Compare that with Margot,
who wants to nurse newborns in Palestine. I still have visions of
gorgeous dresses and fascinating people. As I've told you many
times before, I want to see the world and do all kinds of exciting
things, and a little money won't hurt!*

Well, she was only fourteen when she wrote this, and she
had a right to dream of the good things life might hold. But
this was obviously the daydream of a well-educated girl of
good family, and reveals the social confidence of her class.

Anne Frank has remained a girl to all of us, a girl just becoming a young woman. Yet if she had lived she would be entering her seventies now. What would she have been like?
How would her talents have developed? Which of her dreams
would have come true? Would she have reconciled the contradictions within herself? All these are empty questions—
vain attempts to come closer to a life that was not destined to
be lived. Anne Frank was not yet sixteen years old when she
was murdered.

In his article "A Child's Voice," Jan Romein wrote: "To me the
fate of this Jewish girl epitomizes the worst crime perpetrated

by everlastingly abominable minds. For the worst crime is not the destruction of life and culture as such—these could also fall victim to a culture-creating revolution—but the throttling of the sources of culture, the destruction of life and talent for the mere sake of mindless destructiveness."[75]

# 17 Arrest and Deportation

The diary Anne Frank kept from June 12, 1942, until August 1, 1944, has been read by countless people. They all come to the brief sentence printed after the last entry:

ANNE'S DIARY ENDS HERE

Anne's life, however, did not end there. At this point a kind of life began that we can hardly imagine in all its horror and suffering, and perhaps many of us would rather not try. We know, of course, that Anne Frank died in Bergen-Belsen, but we would prefer to remain ignorant of the details of the seven months she still had left to live after her arrest. Those seven months are part of her life, however. Seven months is a long time when you are fifteen, a very long time. Seven months must seem endless if you are living them in a German concentration camp and have to try to survive from one day to the next. Every day would seem like a lifetime.

"Anne's diary ends here." It ended on August 1, 1944, the date of her last entry. On August 4 Anne and her seven companions in hiding were taken away. We know that they had been betrayed. (Of the twenty-five thousand or more Jews

who went into hiding in the Netherlands between 1940 and
1945, eight to nine thousand fell into the hands of the Germans as a result of raids by the Germans and their Dutch collaborators, or through chance, carelessness, or betrayal.)[76]

To this day no one knows who gave away the eight people in the Secret Annex. After the war, two investigations were carried out into the conduct of one of the company's storeroom workers, but the outcome was insufficient for any charges to be brought. However, we do know the name of the SS sergeant who made the arrest: Karl Silberbauer. Silberbauer had entered the SS in 1939, and until he was transferred to Branch Office IV $B_4$ (the so-called Jewish Section), he served as a policeman in his native city of Vienna, where he went back to work after the war. His conduct was later investigated, too, and evidence from Otto Frank that Silberbauer had obviously been carrying out instructions and had behaved correctly at the time of the arrest is thought to have been crucial in enabling him to return to his old job. Otto Frank was anything but a vengeful man.[77]

On August 4, 1944, Silberbauer was accompanied by some armed Dutch civilians, but it was Silberbauer himself who arrested the Jews in the Secret Annex.

The prisoners were taken to the headquarters of the SS security service and moved a day later to the former internment camp of Westerbork, now a Jewish transit camp. They spent a whole month there. One of the main industries in the Westerbork camp was splitting electric batteries, an occupation that made those engaged in it very dirty and made them cough, because the batteries gave off a substance that irritated the breathing passages.[78] Rachel van Amerongen-Frankfoorder, who was working in the office at Westerbork, says that Otto

**150**   Frank came to her one day and asked her to let Anne work cleaning the camp instead, but unfortunately that was impossible.[79] Presumably Anne, like almost everyone else, was working on the batteries.

Until now weekly transports from Westerbork had been "going East," as the Germans put it. But in August 1944, some weeks after the Allied invasion at Normandy, the prisoners felt safe. They did not think the Germans could deport them to Poland now. However, on September 3, 1944, when the Allies had just reached the southern frontier of the Netherlands, one last transport from Westerbork set out for Auschwitz. All eight Jews from the Secret Annex were on that transport. They were loaded into cattle cars, crammed close together without food and drink or access to a toilet. Only those lucky enough to be near the wall could sometimes crouch down. The journey took three days.

Bloeme Evers-Emden knew Margot and Anne from school; she had been in the same year as Margot. She met the Franks again in Westerbork, and she too was on the last transport. She describes their arrival:

"I can only remember a few things about those countless hours on that train from Westerbork to Auschwitz. I remember we were pressed against one another, not having any room and falling down in sleep—nothing more.

"I do remember the arrival very well. The doors of the cars finally opened and men stood there in blue and white striped outfits. They screamed and kicked us out of the cars. I also remember suddenly seeing a woman talking to one of those people; I concluded that he was someone she knew and then I understood that they were prisoners as well.

"We were taken, with our baggage, to a large area that was

lit up by extraordinarily strong lights—so strong that I had
the feeling that they were moons. I thought, We're on another
planet—that crazy idea fit right into my experience. I think
that that trip had somewhat dulled our awareness, allowing
for thoughts that did not arise from ordinary reality. I
thought, We have arrived on another planet after that trip,
and here there are three moons.

"The place was muddy. Some people stamped their valu-
ables into the ground.

"Then we were taken to rooms where we had to undress.
That was an enormous shock for me. I was eighteen, shy, and
had been brought up chastely, according to the prevailing
morality. It goes without saying that I was embarrassed and
ashamed. I remember an audible crack in my head, from being totally naked before the eyes of men. And then the
thought came like a flash that, from then on, other norms and
values would be in effect, that I would have to adjust to that,
and that an entirely new life was beginning, or death was
waiting."[80]

One thousand and nineteen people in all had come to
Auschwitz on this last transport. Immediately after arrival,
while they were still on the station platform, they were selected. Two hundred and fifty-eight men and two hundred
and twelve women were taken into the camp and had numbers tattooed on the left arm. The other five hundred and
forty-nine people on the transport, including all children under fifteen, were gassed at once.

Families were separated as soon as they arrived. The
women were taken to Women's Camp 29. There are rumors
that Mr. van Pels was one of those gassed immediately after
their arrival. Fritzi Frank's version of the story is that Otto

152 Frank, Mr. van Pels, Peter, and Dr. Pfeffer stayed together in Auschwitz. Peter worked in the post office; the other three were sent to do outdoor labor. After a while, Mr. van Pels injured his thumb and asked the foreman of the working party if he could do indoor work instead the next day. He was given permission. That day men were selected from all the huts to be gassed, and Mr. van Pels was among them.[81]

The second to be murdered was Fritz Pfeffer, who died in Neuengamme concentration camp on December 20, 1944. (There were frequent transfers of prisoners still capable of working from Auschwitz to other camps.) The date of Mrs. van Pels's death is unknown; we know only that she was taken from Auschwitz to Bergen-Belsen, from there to Buchenwald, and then on to Theresienstadt. The Dutch Red Cross gives the time and place of her death as between April 9 and May 8, 1945, in Germany or Czechoslovakia. Peter died in Mauthausen on May 5, 1945, three days before the camp was liberated.

Mrs. Frank, Margot, and Anne were together in Auschwitz-Birkenau. Lenie de Jong van Naarden knew them there. "In the period that we were in Auschwitz—about two months—Mrs. Frank tried very hard to keep her children alive, to keep them with her, to protect them. Naturally, we spoke to each other. But you could do absolutely nothing, only give advice like, 'If they go to the latrine, go with them.' Because even on the way from the barracks to the latrine, something could happen. You might walk in front of an SS man by accident, and your life would be over. They simply beat people to death. It didn't make any difference to them. A human being was nothing."[82]

She also remembers Anne and Margot being put in the scabies block. Mrs. Frank had not eaten her own bread ration but saved it for her children. They dug a hole under the wooden wall of the scabies block, and Margot took the piece of bread and shared it with Anne.

Anne and Margot stayed less than two months in Auschwitz-Birkenau before they were "transferred" to Bergen-Belsen, the concentration camp on the Lüneburg Heath in Germany. Edith Frank was left in Auschwitz, where she died of hunger and exhaustion on January 6, 1945.

Bergen-Belsen was originally regarded as one of the "better" camps, and was also described as an "exchange camp" because it was built for Jews intended to be exchanged for Germans held outside the Nazi sphere of influence. (One such exchange did in fact take place, and is described by Clara Asscher-Pinkhoff in her book *Sternkinder*,[83] and a second was planned, but in all the confusion of the final stages of the war the prisoners never got out of Germany.) A "better" camp was not a concentration camp, or at least people were not systematically murdered there. Conditions changed, however, in the autumn of 1944. When the transports arrived in Bergen-Belsen from Auschwitz-Birkenau in late October and early November, bringing three thousand six hundred and ninety-five women in all (they were "sick, but potentially curable"), there were no new huts ready for them and they had to sleep in severely overcrowded tents, in cold weather. After a week a fall storm swept over the heath and several tents were blown away.

Consequently the camp was overcrowded when Anne and Margot arrived, and the numbers increased. There was no provision for hygiene. The SS could no longer keep order in the increasing chaos, and gradually confined themselves to

**154**   guarding the camp and preventing attempts at escape. Sickness broke out, and, as there were almost no medicines, nothing could be done about it. In particular, the typhus epidemic that broke out at the beginning of 1945 caused about fifty thousand of the hundred and twenty-five thousand Jews in Bergen-Belsen to "perish," by far the majority of them in the last months before the liberation and the first few weeks after it.

Hanneli Goslar, Anne's childhood friend, whom Anne had thought dead already, survived Bergen-Belsen. She says that one day someone told her Anne was in the camp too. The new part of it was separated from hers by barbed wire. Hanneli went to the wire fence and called out to Anne. Someone fetched her. They could not see each other as it was dark and the barbed-wire fence, filled in with straw, was between them, but they talked to each other.

"It wasn't the same Anne. She was a broken girl. I probably was, too, but it was so terrible. She immediately began to cry, and she told me, 'I don't have any parents anymore.'

"I remember that with absolute certainty. That was terribly sad, because she couldn't have known anything else. She thought that her father had been gassed right away. But Mr. Frank looked very young and healthy, and of course the Germans didn't know how old everybody was who they wanted to gas, but selected them on the basis of their appearance. [. . .] I always think, if Anne had known that her father was still alive, she might have had more strength to survive, because she died very shortly before the end—only a few days before [liberation]. But maybe it was all predestined. [. . .] She told me that Margot was seriously ill. [. . .] Then she said, 'We don't have anything at all to eat here, almost nothing, and

we are cold; we don't have any clothes and I've gotten very
thin and they shaved my hair.' "[84]

Hanneli had just received a tiny Red Cross package, the
first since she arrived in the camp a year before. She took
what she had—her friends gave something too—made a
package of it and threw it over the fence for Anne the next
day. But a woman beside Anne grabbed the package and
would not let go of it. Anne was in despair, but Hanneli
promised her another. She managed to throw one over a few
days later, and that was the last time she had any contact with
Anne.

Janny Brandes-Brilleslijper also survived Auschwitz and
Bergen-Belsen, with her sister Lien (who became well-known
later in East Germany as a singer of Yiddish songs under the
name of Lin Jaldati). She says it was very important to be one
of a couple and to feel responsible for another human being.
Janny and Lien worked as nurses in Bergen-Belsen, and Janny
tells us that Anne and Margot fell sick with typhus. At some
time in those last few days Anne was standing in front of her,
wrapped in a blanket. "She didn't have any more tears. Oh,
we hadn't had tears for a long time. And she told me that she
had such a horror of the lice and fleas in her clothes that she
had thrown all of her clothes away. It was the middle of winter and she was wrapped in one blanket. I gathered up everything I could find to give her so that she was dressed again.
We didn't have much to eat, and Lientje was terribly sick, but
I gave Anne some of our bread ration."[85] When Janny looked
for Anne and Margot two days later, they were both dead.

They had typhus, and that had sealed their fate. But it was
not fate; they were murdered with typhus as surely as if someone had killed them with his own hands.

Rachel van Amerongen-Frankfoorder, who was in the same hut as Anne and Margot in Bergen-Belsen, gives the following account of what happened:

"The Frank girls were so emaciated. They looked terrible. They had little squabbles, caused by their illness, because it was clear that they had typhus. You could tell even if you had never had anything to deal with [like] that before. Typhus was the hallmark of Bergen-Belsen. They had those hollowed-out faces, skin over bone. They were terribly cold. They had the least desirable places in the barracks, below, near the door, which was constantly opened and closed. You heard them constantly screaming, 'Close the door, close the door,' and the voices became weaker every day.

"You could really see both of them dying, as well as others. But what was so sad, of course, was that these children were still so young. I always found it so horrible that as children, they had never really lived. They were indeed the youngest among us. The rest of us were all a bit older.

"They showed the recognizable symptoms of typhus—that gradual wasting away, a sort of apathy, with occasional revivals, until they became so sick that there wasn't any hope. And their end came. I don't know which one was carried out earlier, Anne or Margot. Suddenly, I didn't see them anymore, so I had to assume that they had died. Look, I didn't pay any special attention to them because there were so many others who also died. When I didn't see them again, I assumed that they had died there, down there on that bunk. One fine day, they weren't there any longer—actually, a bad day.

"The dead were always carried outside, laid down in front of the barracks, and when you were let out in the morning to go to the latrine, you had to walk past them. That was just as dreadful as going to the latrine itself, because gradually everyone got typhus. In front of the barracks was a kind of wheelbarrow in which you could take care of your needs. Sometimes you also had to take those wheelbarrows to the latrine. Possibly it was on one of those trips to the latrine that I walked past the bodies of the Frank sisters, one or both—I don't know. At the time, I assumed that the bodies of the Frank girls had also been put down in front of the barracks. And then the heaps would be cleared away. A huge hole would be dug and they were thrown into it. That I'm sure of. That must have been their fate, because that's what happened with other people. I don't have a single reason for assuming that it was any different for them than for the other women with us who died at the same time."[86]

Anne's life ended here.

# Postscript

News of the discovery of five previously unpublished pages from Anne Frank's diary broke in the summer of 1998. This find led to worldwide discussion, and of course to arguments between the various people and institutions holding rights to the diary. Journalists wrote articles asking whether a new picture of Anne Frank would now emerge.

The pages themselves consist of two diary entries. One of them, the longer one, is dated February 8, 1944, and has been published in a Dutch newspaper.

In this entry in her diary, Anne Frank writes about her parents' marriage. It has always been held up to her as an ideal partnership, she says; never any quarrels, all sweetness and light. She adds, however, that she knows something about her father's past and can guess the rest. She thinks he married her mother only because he thought she was a suitable woman to be his wife. I quote: *It can't be easy for a woman in love to know she will never come first in her husband's heart.* Anne thinks her mother deserves admiration for never complaining or showing any jealousy, and can see no reason why her father should have married anyone else, for, and I quote again: *His ideals*

**160**   *were gone; his youth was over.* (Otto Frank was actually only thirty-six when he married Edith Holländer, age twenty-five, in 1925!) Anne looks at the way the marriage has turned out. There are no quarrels and no differences of opinion in it, she admits, but she doesn't think it is an ideal marriage either. Her father appreciates her mother's good qualities and is fond of her, but not in the way she, Anne, imagines love between husband and wife.

Otto Frank, Anne continues, accepts her mother as she is, and though he often feels irritation, he says as little as possible because he knows what sacrifices she has had to make. He is not in love with her; he kisses her just as he kisses Anne and Margot. Perhaps, says Anne, it is her mother's great sacrifice that has made her hard and strange. If that were the case, she would be bound to move further and further from real love. Anne goes on to wonder if that means she ought to feel more sympathy for her mother and try to help her. She answers her own question in the negative: no, she can't. Her mother has never confided in her, and she, Anne, has never asked any questions. She just can't talk to her, she can't look lovingly into those cold eyes. If only she was anything like a really understanding mother, writes Anne, if she showed a bit of affection or kindness or patience or something, then she would persevere in trying to get closer to her. I quote again: *But with her unfeeling nature, her sarcastic manner—well, I find it more impossible to love her every day.*

In 1980, the year he died, Otto Frank gave these pages to his friend Cor Suijk of the Anne Frank Foundation in Amsterdam. Presumably he did not want them to be found among his papers after his death. Why not? Probably for the same reasons that he left certain phrases, sentences, and parts

of sentences out of the first published edition of the diary,
passages in which Anne did much less than justice to her
mother and some of her other companions in hiding. From
all accounts, Otto Frank was a cultivated and reserved man,
and it is very easy to understand why he wanted to protect his
wife from Anne's unjustified attack, even after the event.
Edith Frank too had been murdered. No doubt he also felt a
certain loyalty to the other people who had hidden in the Secret Annex. All his life he refused to have a complete edition
of the diary published, although he must have known that
there would be such an edition after his death, and he probably wanted to keep these particularly compromising lines of
Anne's away from public view entirely. Then why not simply
burn them? I think that would have been going too far for
him; he would have felt he was doing his daughter an injury.

The question remains, why has Cor Suijk waited until now
to produce the new pages? When the Netherlands State Institute for War Documentation (RIOD) was preparing the Critical Edition, why did he not say, "I have some further pages,
but Otto Frank did not want them published"? Why come up
with them at this point? Mr. Suijk has said that he wants to
sell them in order to finance the "educational work" of the
Anne Frank Center in New York—a plan that unfortunately
puts the whole affair in a bad light. RIOD hopes to include
the entries in a new edition of the diary and has sought legal
advice on obtaining the pages.

But I do feel sure of one thing: no new picture of Anne
Frank will emerge, although different interpretations may be
placed on her character depending on time, place, and point
of view. The picture of a girl writing, often in desperation, to
fend off loneliness and inhumanity will endure. And if Anne

•

# Postscript

162   is used as a weapon against inhumanity, if quotations are taken from her diary to encourage us to love our fellow human beings in spite of everything, what harm can there be in that?

Looking at the whole Anne Frank debate, I think it is a pity so little attention has been paid to the period of her life that began with the family's arrest. Discussion of the book, particularly in schools, should not conclude with the words "Anne's diary ends here." It ought to go further.

*Mirjam Pressler*
*October 1998*

# Chronology

**JUNE 12, 1929:** Annelies Marie Frank, known as Anne, born in Frankfurt. (Her sister, Margot, was born on February 16, 1926.)

**1933:** Adolf Hitler assumes power. The first laws discriminating against Jews are passed. Over the next few years more and more laws deprive the Jewish part of the German population of their civil rights. Otto Frank emigrates to Amsterdam and starts a company there. His wife, Edith, and Margot follow at the end of the year, and Anne joins them in February 1934.

**NOVEMBER 9–10, 1938:** Organized pogroms take place throughout Germany ("Crystal Night").

**SEPTEMBER 1, 1939:** The Second World War begins with the German attack on Poland.

**1939–1940:** Deportations of Jews to ghettos and concentration camps begin.

**MAY 10, 1940:** Occupation of the Netherlands by German troops. Anti-Jewish laws come into force in the Netherlands over the following year.

**SEPTEMBER 1, 1941:** Wearing of the yellow Star of David by Jews is made compulsory in Germany, and from May 1942 in the Netherlands as well.

**DECEMBER 1941:** Beginning of the mass extermination of Jews.

**DECEMBER 20, 1941:** The "final solution of the Jewish problem" is decided at the Wannsee Conference: Jews are to be decimated by forced labor done on an inadequate diet, and "the requisite treatment" is to be given to the "remaining stock."

**JUNE 1942:** The first mass gassings in Auschwitz.

**JUNE 16, 1942:** Anne is given an autograph album for her thirteenth birthday and begins to keep a diary.

**JULY 5, 1942:** A call-up notice arrives for Margot to report for labor duties in the east. The next day the Frank family moves into a hiding place prepared at 263 Prinsengracht. The van Pels family joins them on July 13.

**NOVEMBER 16, 1942:** Fritz Pfeffer moves into the Secret Annex.

# Chronology

**JUNE 6, 1944:** Beginning of the Allied invasion.

**AUGUST 4, 1944:** Arrest of the eight people in hiding, and their helpers Kleiman and Kugler.

**SEPTEMBER 3, 1944:** All eight are on the last transport from Westerbork to Auschwitz. They arrive on September 6. Mrs. Frank, Anne, and Margot are taken to the women's camp of Auschwitz-Birkenau. Soon after arriving, Mr. van Pels dies in the gas chamber. Fritz Pfeffer dies in Neuengamme concentration camp on December 20. The date of Mrs. van Pels's death is not known. Peter survives an "evacuation march" from Auschwitz to the concentration camp of Mauthausen, where he dies on May 5, 1945.

**LATE OCTOBER OR EARLY NOVEMBER 1944:** Anne and Margot are taken to the concentration camp of Bergen-Belsen. Edith Frank is left in Auschwitz-Birkenau, where she dies on January 6, 1945.

**JANUARY 27, 1945:** Auschwitz concentration camp is liberated by the Red Army. Otto Frank is among the survivors.

**LATE FEBRUARY TO EARLY MARCH 1945:** Anne and Margot die of typhus in Bergen-Belsen.

**1947:** First Dutch edition of Anne's diary published under the title *Het Achterhuis*.

**1950:** First German edition of the diary published as *Das Tagebuch der Anne Frank*, translated by Annelies Schütz.

**1952:** First English edition of the diary published as *The Diary of a Young Girl* in the United States and Britain, translated by Mrs. B. M. Mooyart-Doubleday.

**1980:** Otto Frank dies on August 19 at Birsfelden in Switzerland.

**1986:** The Netherlands State Institute for War Documentation publishes the Critical Edition of Anne's diary as *The Diary of Anne Frank*, with the English version using Mrs. Mooyart-Doubleday's translation and additional passages translated by Arnold J. Pomerans.

**1991:** Extended new edition (the Definitive Edition), edited and translated by Mirjam Pressler, published in Germany as *Anne Frank. Tagebuch*.

**1995:** The Definitive Edition published by Doubleday in the United States as *The Diary of a Young Girl*, in a new translation by Susan Massotty.

**1997:** The Definitive Edition in Susan Massotty's translation published in the UK by Viking.

**1998:** Discovery of new, previously unknown pages from Anne Frank's diary.

# Notes

1. *Die Auschwitz-Hefte*, Beltz Verlag, Weinheim, 1987, vol. 2, p. 261ff.
2. Later on, these documents were handed to the commission investigating Nazi crimes in Cracow, and Dr. Otto Wolken explained what his secret notes meant. Some of them are reproduced in Friedrich Karl Kraul, *Ärzte in Auschwitz,* Berlin, 1968.
3. Crematorium IV had been blown up on October 7, 1944, during a revolt by members of the "Special Commando" (Jewish prisoners forced to take corpses out of the gas chambers and transport them to the crematoria). Four hundred and fifty Special Commandos escaped but were recaptured and shot. On Himmler's orders the other crematoria were progressively dismantled as the Red Army approached, beginning in November 1944. On January 20, 1945, the SS blew up the remains of Crematoria II and III, which had already been largely demolished, and Crematorium V was blown up on January 26. (I have found no records of Crematorium I; it may have been the "old crematorium" in the main Auschwitz camp.)
4. Rudolf Höss, camp commander of Auschwitz from May 1, 1940, gave evidence under oath at Nuremberg on April 5, 1946. He said at the trial that he had commanded Auschwitz until December 1, 1943, and estimated that at least "2,500,000 victims were executed and exterminated by gassing and burning, and at least another half million succumbed to starvation and disease, making a total of about 3,000,000." This figure, he added, represented about 70 or 80 percent of all prisoners sent to Auschwitz; the rest were selected for slave labor in the concentration camp industries. Among those executed were approximately 20,000 Russian prisoners of war. The rest of the victims comprised some 100,000 German Jews and a great many mainly Jewish nationals from Holland, France, Belgium, Poland, Hungary, Czechoslovakia, Greece,

# Notes

and other countries. "Another improvement we made over Treblinka was that we built our gas chambers to accommodate 2,000 people at once, whereas at Treblinka their ten gas chambers only accommodated 200 people each." (Gerhard Schoenberger, *Der gelbe Stern: Die Judenverfolgung in Europa* ("The yellow star: the persecution of Jews in Europe"), C. Bertelsmann Verlag, Munich, 1978, p. 136; quotations in English from William L. Shirer, *The Rise and Fall of the Third Reich,* Secker & Warburg, London, 1960).

5. *Brockhaus Enzyklopädie,* 19th edition, F. A. Brockhaus, Mannheim, 1986.

6. Martin Gilbert, *Auschwitz and the Allies,* Michael Joseph, London, 1981, p. 337.

7. Elfriede (Fritzi) Frank (Otto Frank's second wife) in a letter to the author.

8. K. Zetnik, *Di Schwue,* I. L. Peretz Publishing, Tel Aviv, 1982.

9. Quoted from Ernst Schnabel, *Anne Frank: Spur eines Kindes,* Fischer Bücherei KG, Frankfurt am Main, 1958.

10. Quoted from Miep Gies (with Alison Leslie Gold), *Anne Frank Remembered,* Simon & Schuster Inc., New York, 1987, p. 231.

11. Willy Lindwer, *The Last Seven Months of Anne Frank,* Anchor Books, Doubleday, Bantam Doubleday Dell, New York, 1992, pp. 83–84.

12. Miep Gies, *Anne Frank Remembered,* p. 235.

13. Unless there is an indication to the contrary, most of the passages printed in italics are taken from the new Definitive Edition (Anne Frank, *The Diary of a Young Girl,* edited by Otto H. Frank and Mirjam Pressler; English translation by Susan Massotty, Doubleday, New York, 1995). When quotations are from the English-language version of the scholarly Critical Edition (*The Diary of Anne Frank,* edited by David Barnouw and Gerard van der Stroom; English translation by Arnold J. Pomerans, Doubleday, 1989), the fact is indicated. There are also references to and a quotation from Anne Frank's collection of stories, originally published in 1949 in Dutch as *Verhaaltjes en Gebeurtenissen uit her Achterhuis;* English translation, *Tales from the House Behind,* The World's Work, 1952; complete English version, *Tales from the Secret Annex,* translated by Michel Mok and Ralph Manheim, Doubleday, 1983.

14. See also *Tales from the Secret Annex,* pp. 62–65.

15. Critical Edition, p. 59.

16. Critical Edition, p. 62.

17. Published in *Het Parool,* April 3, 1946. Critical Edition, p. 67.

18. Critical Edition, p. 237.

19. Critical Edition, p. 238.

20. Critical Edition, p. 240.

21. These facts, and other information in this chapter, are taken from the

very illuminating exhibition catalog by Jürgen Steen and Wolf von **167**
Wolzogen, *Anne Frank aus Frankfurt* ("Anne Frank of Frankfurt"), Historisches Museum Frankfurt, Frankfurt, 1990. See p. 12 of this catalog.

22. Steen and von Wolzogen, *Anne Frank aus Frankfurt*, p. 26.
23. According to the letter notifying them that they had to leave (Steen and von Wolzogen, *Anne Frank aus Frankfurt*, p. 58).
24. Steen and von Wolzogen, *Anne Frank aus Frankfurt*, p. 67.
25. This was the Law for the Reconstitution of the Civil Service, which entailed the dismissal of all civil servants of non-Aryan descent (Steen and von Wolzogen, *Anne Frank aus Frankfurt*, p. 64).
26. Information in this chapter is taken from Mozes Heiman Gans, *Memorboek: Platenatlas van het leven der joden in Nederland van de middeleeuwen tot 1940*, Bosch & Keuning n.v., Baarn, 6th edition, 1988.
27. Gans, *Memorboek*, p. 28.
28. Steen and von Wolzogen, *Anne Frank aus Frankfurt*, p. 74.
29. Volker Jacob and Annet van der Voort, eds., *Anne Frank war nicht allein: Lebensgeschichten deutscher Juden in den Niederlanden* ("Anne Frank was not alone: the experiences of German Jews in the Netherlands"), Dietz, Berlin, 1988, p. 19.
30. Lindwer, *The Last Seven Months of Anne Frank*, pp. 11–34.
31. Miep Gies, *Anne Frank Remembered*, p. 33.
32. Quoted in Lindwer, *The Last Seven Months of Anne Frank*, p. 17.
33. Miep Gies, *Anne Frank Remembered*, p. 39.
34. Critical Edition, p. 177.
35. Miep Gies, *Anne Frank Remembered*, p. 46.
36. Miep Gies, *Anne Frank Remembered*, p. 56.
37. Critical Edition, p. 207.
38. Miep Gies, *Anne Frank Remembered*, p. 115.
39. Miep Gies, *Anne Frank Remembered*, p. 245.
40. Miep Gies, *Anne Frank Remembered*, p. 37.
41. Miep Gies, *Anne Frank Remembered*, p. 31.
42. Miep Gies, *Anne Frank Remembered*, p. 133.
43. Miep Gies, *Anne Frank Remembered*, p. 166.
44. Miep Gies, *Anne Frank Remembered*, p. 166.
45. Miep Gies, *Anne Frank Remembered*, p. 165.
46. Miep Gies, *Anne Frank Remembered*, p. 114. (Miep Gies uses Anne Frank's pseudonyms for some of the Secret Annex residents. To avoid confusion, real names are used here and elsewhere.)
47. Miep Gies, *Anne Frank Remembered*, p. 37.
48. Miep Gies, *Anne Frank Remembered*, p. 133ff.
49. Miep Gies, *Anne Frank Remembered*, p. 133.
50. Miep Gies, *Anne Frank Remembered*, p. 136.
51. Miep Gies, *Anne Frank Remembered*, p. 104.
52. J. Presser, *Ondergang: De vervolging en verdelging van het Nederlandse jo-*

# Notes

dendom, 1940–1945, Staatsuitgeverij's-Gravenhage, 1985, vol. 2, facing p. 177.

53. Miep Gies, *Anne Frank Remembered*, p. 30.
54. Schnabel, *Anne Frank: Spur eines Kindes,* p. 80.
55. Miep Gies, *Anne Frank Remembered*, p. 55.
56. Miep Gies, *Anne Frank Remembered*, p. 147.
57. Schnabel, *Anne Frank: Spur eines Kindes,* p. 74.
58. Miep Gies, *Anne Frank Remembered*, p. 53.
59. According to information provided by Vincent Frank-Steiner, former chairman of the Anne Frank Foundation, Basel.
60. Miep Gies, *Anne Frank Remembered,* p. 187. (In her book, Miep Gies uses the pseudonyms generally employed earlier for the helpers. To avoid confusion, the real names Kleiman and Jan are given in this quotation instead of the pseudonyms Koophuis and Henk.)
61. Miep Gies, *Anne Frank Remembered,* p. 88.
62. From information in the Critical Edition, p. 55ff. Miep Gies, however, writes that "in fact he had escaped from the hands of the Germans and had been hiding in his own home, through the Hunger Winter, cared for by his wife" (*Anne Frank Remembered*, p. 229).
63. *Meyers Lexikon,* revised edition, Bibliographisches Institut, Mannheim, 1983.
64. Schoenberger, *Der gelbe Stern,* p. 216.
65. Gilbert, *Auschwitz and the Allies,* p. 35.
66. Hans-Dieter Schmidt *et al., Juden unterm Hakenkreuz: Dokumente und Berichte zur Verfolgung und Vernichtung der Juden durch die National-sozialisten, 1933–1945* ("Jews under the Swastika: documents and testimony of the Nazi persecution and extermination of Jews, 1933–1945"), Schwann, Düsseldorf, 1983, vol. 2, p. 127.
67. Gilbert, *Auschwitz and the Allies,* p. 42ff.
68. Critical Edition, p. 276, version A.
69. *Tales from the Secret Annex,* p. 135ff.
70. Lindwer, *The Last Seven Months of Anne Frank,* p. 14.
71. Lindwer, *The Last Seven Months of Anne Frank,* p. 15.
72. *Tales from the Secret Annex,* p. 44ff.
73. Critical Edition, p. 191.
74. See also the story "Why?" in *Tales from the Secret Annex,* p. 143ff.
75. Critical Edition, p. 67.
76. These facts and other information in this chapter are taken from the Critical Edition.
77. Otto Frank's sense of responsibility toward others was evident even after his return from Auschwitz. Fritzi Frank says he sought out survivors, helped them, cared for orphaned children, and reunited them with their relations. Until his death in 1980 he used a large part of the fortune he acquired through the success of Anne's diary to provide fi-

nancial support for other people, in particular victims of the Nazi
regime.

78. Lindwer, *The Last Seven Months of Anne Frank,* p. 52.
79. Lindwer, *The Last Seven Months of Anne Frank,* p. 92.
80. Lindwer, *The Last Seven Months of Anne Frank,* pp. 120–121.
81. Elfriede Frank (Otto Frank's second wife) in a letter of September 22, 1992, to the author.
82. Lindwer, *The Last Seven Months of Anne Frank,* p. 153.
83. Clara Asscher-Pinkhoff, *Sternkinder* ("Children of the star"), Oetinger, Hamburg, 1986.
84. Lindwer, *The Last Seven Months of Anne Frank,* pp. 27–28.
85. Lindwer, *The Last Seven Months of Anne Frank,* p. 74.
86. Lindwer, *The Last Seven Months of Anne Frank,* pp. 104–105.

# Bibliography

## OF BOOKS NOT EXPLICITLY MENTIONED IN THE NOTES

Adler, H. G., et al. *Auschwitz: Zeugnisse und Berichte*. Cologne: Europäische Verlagsanstalt, 1984.

Gebhardt, Bruno. *Handbuch der deutschen Geschichte*. 22 vols. Munich: Deutscher Taschenbuch Verlag, 1980.

Gilbert, Gustave M. *Nürnberger Tagebuch: Gespräche der Angeklagten mit dem Gerichtspsychologen*. Frankfurt am Main: Fischer Taschenbuch Verlag, 1987.

Pätzold, Kurt, ed. *Verfolgung, Vertreibung, Vernichtung*. Frankfurt am Main: Röderberg-Verlag, 1984.

Schuder, Rosemarie, and Rudolf Hirsch. *Der gelbe Fleck: Wurzeln und Wirkungen des Judenhassees in der deutschen Geschichte*. Berlin: Rütten & Loening, 1987.

# Acknowledgments

The publishers wish to thank the following for permission to reproduce copyrighted material. All possible care has been taken to trace the ownership of all material included and to make full acknowledgments for its use. If any errors have accidentally occurred, they will be corrected in subsequent printings, provided notification is sent to the publishers.

*The Diary of Anne Frank: The Critical Edition*, prepared by the Netherlands State Institute for War Documentation, edited by David Barnouw and Gerard Van Der Stroom, translated by Arnold J. Pomerans (Viking/Doubleday, 1989, first published as *Da Dagboeken van Anne Frank* by Staatsuitgeverij's-Gravenhage and Uitgeverij Bert Bakker, Amsterdam). Copyright © 1986 by Rijksinstituut voor Oorlogsdocumentatie, Amsterdam, the Netherlands, for preface, introduction, commentary, notes; English translation copyright © 1989 by Doubleday, a division of Random House, Inc., and by Penguin Books Ltd. Reproduced by permission of the Anne Frank-Fonds, Basel, Switzerland, and Penguin Books Ltd.

*The Diary of a Young Girl: The Definitive Edition* by Anne Frank, edited by Otto H. Frank and Mirjam Pressler, translated by Susan Massotty (Doubleday, 1995). Copyright © The Anne Frank-Fonds, Basel, Switzerland, 1991. English translation copyright © Doubleday, a division of Random House, Inc., 1995. Reproduced by permission of Doubleday and Penguin Books Ltd.

*Anne Frank Remembered* by Miep Gies and Alison Leslie Gold. Copyright © 1987 Miep Gies and Alison Leslie Gold. Used by permission of Simon & Schuster, Inc.

# Acknowledgments

172   *Anne Frank's Tales from the Secret Annex*, translated by Michel Mok and Ralph Manheim. Used by permission of Doubleday, and also the Anne Frank-Fonds, Basel, Switzerland.

*The Last Seven Months of Anne Frank* by Willy Lindwer. Copyright © 1988 by Willy Lindwer; English translation copyright © 1991 by Random House, Inc. Used by permission of Pantheon Books, a division of Random House, Inc.

All interior photographs are copyright © The Anne Frank-Fonds, Basel, and Cosmopress, Geneva, and are used by permission.

All jacket photographs are copyright © The Anne Frank-Fonds, Basel/Anne Frank Stichting, Amsterdam.

# Index

# Index

# Index